Paulette + Jim

God bless

Ralph

TO YOU, MY GRANDCHILDREN

Ralph E. Vaughn

Erin Thurman, Austin Hawkins, Ralph Vaughn, Drake Vaughn

Write Together™ Publishing
Nashville, Tennessee

Published by Write Together Publishing ™ LLC.
www.writetogether.com

ISBN   1-931718-06-7 Paperback

Title: To You, My Grandchildren.
Author: Ralph E. Vaughn
Subject: Memoirs, Local History
All photographs by Linda D. Vaughn

For Write Together Publishing:

Publisher: Paul Clere

Edit: John D. Bauman

Book Design: Bill Perkins

_____

To publish a book for your school or non-profit organization that complements
your academic goals or values, vision and mission, please contact:

Write Together ™ Publishing
533 Inwood Dr.
Nashville, TN 37211

phone: 615-781-1518
fax: 520-223-4850
www.writetogether.com

Table of Contents

Preface

When I first began to write *To You, My Grandchildren*, it was simply a personal project. I wanted to reach into my mind and rediscover facts from my past and draw from them what I believe to be "lessons in living."

I thought, maybe my experiences will be enlightening to my grandchildren years from now when they read about their grandfather. But I never intended to publish.

My desire was to put on paper emotions from my heart and soul with all the human frailties that make me who I am. Maybe my short stories could be kept in a file or notebook and shared when someone asked about that person whose name is Ralph Vaughn. Again, there was no intention to publish.

In late 2000, I called my friend Steve McKinney and requested an appointment. He is the director of the Boys & Girls Clubs of Rutherford County, Tennessee. When we were together, I told Steve, "I want to do something significant to benefit other people. When I resigned as president from the Rutherford County Chamber of Commerce in 1997, I vowed to myself that life would take on a low profile. But I want to concentrate on doing things that are, in my opinion, significant."

My whole adult life has been relatively high profile. For twenty-one years, I was in the media: radio, television, and newspaper. Then I was president of the Chamber of Commerce for nearly twelve years. During those two careers, my opinions were quoted in the *Wall Street Journal* and *New York Times*. I have appeared on national television and radio and have received a few compliments along the way.

I tell people that I have never had a job in my life. A job is when you must do something you don't want to do, wishing the whole time you were anywhere else. I, however, have been blessed with two careers that I enjoyed immensely, and then I began a third career in November 1997.

Steve responded, "The Boys & Girls Clubs center in Murfreesboro, Tennessee, serves nearly 300 children. We have a temporary facility to serve children in the neighboring towns of LaVergne and Smyrna, but the facility is now overcrowded. No more children can be added to the program until better facilities are created. We plan to launch a capital campaign and build a new center to benefit the children of LaVergne and Smyrna."

I quickly remarked, "I'm not sure what I can do, but I want to help." A few days after that meeting, a burning desire surfaced from my soul. I decided to publish my book.

All profits from the sale of *To You, My Grandchildren* will be given to the Boys & Girls Clubs to endow its programs, and I personally will share my resources to promote a literacy program that helps develop basic reading and writing skills in young people.

Another purpose of this book is to leave as a legacy to my grandchildren my lifetime habit of collecting sayings, anecdotes and little life lessons that I call "punches." The punches included in this work have come from a variety of sources—books, magazines, conversations, and my own life experience—and have been gathered for over thirty years. I hope these punches will act as a guide for better living for my grandchildren and for you, the Reader.

My Creator knows my desire. I believe He will honor this effort "to make the world a better place for His purpose."

With my love for God and my grandchildren, I present *To You, My Grandchildren.*

Chapter 1:

To You, My Grandchildren

To You, My Grandchildren is a venue for me to share with you and future generations some of the "lessons in living" that I learned through either personal experiences or observations. I became committed to writing this project following a conversation in 1991 with my mother, Betty Mae Cantrell Vaughn Wilson.

"Mother, I remember you saying that you were only nine-years-old when your father [William George Cantrell] passed away," I commented. "He was only 39 at the time of his death. Obviously, I'll never know my grandfather. Will you tell me more about him?" We spent the next several minutes talking about her father, my grandfather.

That brief conversation with Mother made me aware of the importance of documenting our experiences for the benefit of others who will follow in our footsteps. *To You, My Grandchildren* was then born.

How should it be written? That was my first question. I decided to begin by taking time out regularly for musing, or reminiscing. While taking a journey through my mind, I write. As I recall experiences, I ask questions: What can I learn from this? Is there a lesson in living? Is there something worth passing on to my grandchildren?

I want you, my grandchildren, to know me. Please take the time to see my strengths, my limitations, and my perceptions. Please laugh with me, and even at me, for some of the silly growing pains I experienced. As you listen to my heart being expressed through these words, you may possibly hear something that will help you live a more productive and positive life. Remember, life is a journey, not a destination.

To You, My Grandchildren

I believe that every person should have a Mission Statement, a statement about what he/she is striving to accomplish. The following is my Mission Statement:

> To help make the world a better place. To improve my mind and to deepen my appreciation for life on a daily basis.

How can a person make the world a better place? I believe the starting point is having an "attitude of gratitude." It is recorded in the Bible that we should pray without ceasing, or have an attitude of prayer. I think that means being keenly aware of God and people. If I want to make the world a better place, then opportunities will certainly come my way. The important thing for me to remember is "attitude."

Attitude will give a person's mind a thirst for knowledge and an appreciation for what life offers. For example, take the time to read, to observe others, to enjoy a beautiful sunrise or a flock of wild geese in flight, or to hear the laughter of a loved one or a friend. It all begins with attitude.

Writing this has already brought me tremendous entertainment and a new awareness of who I am. Golf, fishing and running are good hobbies for some folks. I, however, enjoy playing with words.

As I write and explore the hills and valleys in my mind, I am amazed by the extra energy I feel, perhaps similar to a runner's high. One particular evening I experienced two years in just two hours, minus some of the details, of course.

Musing over past events or about former acquaintances sparks emotions within me that are similar to those I felt at the original time. For example, I remember the old peddling truck that came to our neighborhood when I was a child. While recalling the peddler and his wares, I can still see the twinkle in his eyes as he explained a new, improved product on the market, or as he reported on current events. Even the smell of the old peddling truck is still in my mind after these many years.

My desire is for this to be entertaining for me and to provide future generations a few examples of what life was like in the 20th century. I dedicate this book to my mother, who helped lay the foundation for the character that my life is built on.

Chapter 2: Heritage

My Mother

Permit me to share some thoughts about my mother, the former Betty Mae Cantrell, a real hero. She probably doesn't consider anything she has ever done to be heroic. In my opinion, however, her name should be listed along with those of Washington, Lincoln and Roosevelt. Those incredible men helped shape the destiny of America. Betty Mae, an incredible lady, helped to shape my destiny with her sacrificial love and spiritual guidance.

She taught me the importance of attending church and the value of telling the truth. "You can sleep better at night when you tell the truth," she insisted. I took her at her word; and besides, I wanted to sleep well at night to avoid confronting the strange creatures that prowl after dark. There were a few nights when I woke and became frightened by the howls, hoots and creaky sounds. My escape was to pull the bed covers tightly over my head and then succumb to Mr. Sandman.

As a youngster, the business of telling the truth became my personal obsession. I wouldn't dare repeat a story unless there was no doubt about the origin. I was even afraid to tease my playmates about things that were not absolute. I confess to backsliding a few times when a little white lie escaped from my lips. There was no need to point an accusing finger; I immediately became riddled with guilt.

Apparently God gives mothers extrasensory perception because my mother could always tell when something weighed heavily on my mind. "What's wrong, son?" Mother would inquire.

"Oh, it's nothing," I would respond. She knew better.

"Please tell me, I'll understand," she would then say with reassurance. Mother always listened patiently as I agonized over every minute detail. When I had completely emptied my soul, she ten-

3

derly placed her arms around me and comforted me with these words: "Son, the Lord sees everything. He understands. It's because He knows your heart."

Outward appearances are often misleading. That is a fact as I recall the touch of my mother's hands. Those hands were the ones that stroked my face to wipe away a tear. They were the same hands that pulled me close while reassuring me that everything would be all right and that little boys really recover from skinned knees and broken hearts.

Her hands could literally perform miracles. They truly conveyed a touch of God. Those memories are imprinted so clearly in my mind now as I recall those bumps and bruises from my growing up years.

The hands I remember were different from what others may have seen. Others would have been misled by what only the eyes could see. Long hours of working in the fields made those hands callused. The winter weather also took its toll. I recall the cracked fingers and the bruises that no amount of lotion could smooth.

I am sure that she was embarrassed for others to see her hands, especially when she was at church or in the company of unfamiliar people. It is interesting that I am now thinking about her hands. They were always rough looking but I found them to be full of strength and love.

I believe a God-fearing mother has the ability to calm a frustrated spirit, give courage to a troubled soul, cool a burning fever, and to laugh the loudest when one of her own reaches a goal. I should know. My precious mother has done them all. I am thankful for the gentleness of her touch.

My Father

Have you ever wondered what fathers are supposed to be? The easy answers are a person who sets a good example, a bread winner, a disciplinarian, and a confidant. Those may be easy answers, but they are tough standards for any of us to live up to. Most children, including me when I was young, expect their fathers to be bigger and better than all others.

I thought about my father today while driving near Snow Hill Baptist Church in Smithville. My father was buried there in 1971 following his untimely death, the result of a traffic accident. He was 50 years old.

Who was J.D. Vaughn? He went by the name J.D. and always discounted the possibility that those initials stood for the names of his grandfathers, Jasper "Jappy" Vaughn and David Adcock. I don't think I would like being called Jappy David.

When I was a small lad, my eyes saw him as a tough disciplinarian and the strongest man in the world with enough hair on his chest to make a bear skin rug. I secretly thought that having a hairy chest and a dark beard was the epitome of masculinity. Anything less was to be a sissy, I thought back then.

The older I grew, the more human J.D. Vaughn became. He could get mad like anyone else and say a few choice words like "hell" and "damn," but I don't recall him ever using God's name in a disrespectful way.

He had a major problem that I saw manifested only during the last four years of his life. He had a problem known as alcoholism that actually began when he was a teenager. My mother said he swore off the bottle when I was about four, when he found the grace of God through Christian salvation. Apparently the addiction is always present with an alcoholic. He fought back the desire for about 20 years but then gave in to its subtle and insidious appeal.

As I think about him now, I remember the good qualities of J.D. Vaughn and some principles he shared with me. He taught that I should always do more work than was expected of me, or for what I was due to be paid. He told me to always go the extra mile for another person.

I remember one day when James Ervin, a fellow tippler, was at

5

my parents' home. Dad insisted that I should drive James into Smithville, a distance of about five miles. I was upset that James and Dad had been gone from home all night, presumably on a drinking binge, and I really didn't care if James had to walk every step of the way. Dad continued to insist, so I agreed to drive James home.

As we neared where James lived, my passenger suggested that it would be perfectly all right for him to get out of the car and walk the short distance from Short Mountain Highway to his house located on Hayes Street. Besides, I decided, there was a grocery store at the intersection and James would really prefer to get out there.

Later, Dad asked if I got James home safely, and I responded in the affirmative. I casually mentioned that he actually got out of the car at Foster's Market, maybe a few hundred feet from his house. Dad quickly snapped, "You should have driven him to the front door! Remember son, you are to always go the extra mile."

My Stepfather

C.W. Wilson was another special man in my life. He came on the scene less than a year following my father's death. He won my approval the day he said, "I love your mother and have asked her to marry me. I will never take the place of your father. Don't expect me to. But give me a chance to become your friend." Although I promised never to compare him to my father, I did– from the way he dressed to how he managed the farm.

His manner of dressing was always interesting to me. I saw him many times working on a tractor or performing a dirty farm task. He would be covered from head to toe in dirt and grease. However, when he cleaned up for church, a social visit, or to just go into town, he wore only his finest, complete with coat and tie.

He was sometimes stubborn and always ultra-conservative. I bet he would drive five miles to save a dime but would give me almost anything if there was a need. Before his health began to fail, he earned his due by the sweat of the brow. Hard work was his way of life. It was sad to see him become unable to enjoy life in the manner to which he was accustomed. He had Parkinson's disease for nearly ten years before his death.

C.W. Wilson was a gentle man. I have never known a person more tenderhearted. He cried when I reminded him how much he was loved. That emotion probably stemmed from his never having any children of his own. His Christian faith was exemplary. I have seen him cry while encouraging a "lost soul" to enter the fold. I admired his compassion for others.

While still healthy, he and Mother were daily visitors to area nursing homes, hospitals and funeral homes. Providing encouragement and support to the hurt and lonely was their way of life for many years.

Yes, he was a good man, one who loved from the heart. His example of values and principle is worthy of emulation. In his own way, C.W. Wilson made a statement about life. I like what he said.

Chapter 3:

Punches on Success

Success will not come to you. You must go for it.

•

You can never be a winner by complaining.

•

Act enthusiastic and you will be enthusiastic.

•

Expect to win.

•

Some people say that luck is needed for success. Yet the harder you work, the more luck you will enjoy.

•

You will be as happy and successful as you allow yourself to be.

•

Success is mental, not physical.

•

Control your mind and unleash your mental powers to produce success in every area of your life.

•

Set your sights on success.

•

Some people want it to happen. Some wish it would happen. Others make it happen.

•

The one who complains about the way the ball bounces is likely the one who dropped it.

To You, My Grandchildren

Success is a journey, not a destination.

•

Become a success one step at a time.

•

Create a success philosophy.

•

Few people, if any, come anywhere near to exhausting the strength and resources within them.

•

For every challenge, there is an opportunity.

•

You never get a second chance to make a first impression.

•

The greatest ability is dependability.

•

Avoid just following the crowd.

•

Common sense is just about the most uncommon thing there is.

•

No one is ever defeated until defeat has been accepted as a reality.

•

Success comes to those who become success-conscious.

•

Set your goal to be the best at anything you do.

•

Persist until you succeed.

•

Good habits are the key to success.

•

Today, multiply your value a hundredfold.

•

The secret to persuading others to follow you is to exercise the courage to say exactly what you mean.

•

When you have a passion for something, just thinking about it is enough to tune you in.

•

Think ahead. Think about doing more.

To You, My Grandchildren

Never give up.

•

Celebrate and reward yourself for accomplishments.

•

Believe that you are worthy of greatness.

•

It has been said that eighty percent of success is just showing up.

•

When you reach a goal, congratulate yourself.

•

Take pride in what you do. It will guide you to success.

•

Knowledge is power.

•

Being focused is essential to becoming successful.

•

Wake the sleeping giant inside you. You have more potential than you can ever imagine.

•

You can have more than you've got because you can become more than you are.

•

To create success, you must first believe that you deserve it.

•

Have a mission for your life.

•

Don't wait for an appropriate time to do good. Do it now.

•

Obstacles are disguised opportunities for creativity.

•

Use your talents. Never minimize them.

•

If you get knocked on your back, remember that if you can look up, you can get up.

•

Experience is one thing that doesn't come on an easy payment plan.

11

•

No matter where you are, get the most out of yourself.

To You, My Grandchildren

What you are, not who your father was, is what counts.

•

Look for the potential in every situation.

•

Every person is the architect and builder of his life.

•

Setting the world on fire requires burning some midnight oil.

•

You have a right to be successful.

•

*Invent better ways to do things with your imagination,
rather than just with your efforts.*

•

*The only person who never makes a mistake is the one who
never does anything.*

•

*Count on yourself first, then you can't blame others when things
go wrong.*

•

*Be proud of yourself.
Never in history has there been anyone like you.*

•

*The purpose of life is to matter, to count, to stand for something,
to make a difference, and to show that you lived at all.*

•

*Problems represent challenges that can bring out the
best in you.*

•

*It's not necessarily what you are going to do tomorrow, but what you
are doing today that is important.*

•

*What a surprise to discover that you can do what you were afraid you
couldn't do.*

•

*The most valuable things in life are those that result from hard work
and dedication.*

•

A great person is a servant not a master.

•

12 *Experience is not what happens to you. It is what you do with what
happens to you.*

To You, My Grandchildren

If we didn't have a problem, we wouldn't be alive.

•

Search for excellence every day.

Rest not on past success but move to the next opportunity.

•

Think big. Set your creative mind on fire.

•

Dealing with frustration and rejection requires an effort.

•

We are special. We are engineered for greatness and designed for accomplishment.

•

Learn to know and understand yourself, your skills, your weaknesses, and accept yourself.

•

Enthusiasm can make the difference between success and failure. To be enthusiastic, act enthusiastically.

•

One of the best ways to get self-confidence is to do exactly what you are afraid of doing.

•

Your attitude toward money is more important than how much of it you have.

•

Winning is taking the talent or potential you were born with and using it fully.

•

It's not what you are in life that holds you back. It is what you think you are not.

•

A rebuff is tough; but remember, it can bring out your deeper qualities.

•

You become successful the moment you start moving toward a worthwhile goal.

•

Don't nurse the rejection or curse it. Don't even rehearse it. Immerse it by doing good yourself. Hotheads never produce cool thoughts.

To You, My Grandchildren

It is better to try something good and fail than attempt to do nothing and succeed.

•

The big challenge is to become all that you have the possibility of becoming. You cannot believe what it does to the human spirit to maximize your human potential and stretch yourself to the limit.

14

Chapter 4: Boyhood

A Cold Night on the Farm

For the past several minutes, I have been sitting in front of my fireplace. Watching the fire and hearing the snapping sounds evoke an ambiance of peacefulness. As my eyes were becoming a little heavy, my mind took a journey back in time.

The year was 1957 and the place was our small farm near Smithville. Middle Tennessee was being held firmly in the grip of a winter storm. The scene I remember occurred about 5:30 p.m. Dad and I had just returned to the house after finishing our chores at the barn, feeding and milking our dairy cows by hand.

We quickly made our way to the living room, shaking two hours of numbness from our bodies by wrapping ourselves around the Ashley wood burning heater. Mother was in the kitchen about ready to serve one of my favorite wintertime meals: hot cornbread and a large glass of sweet milk.

On this particular night, because of the extreme cold weather and the fact that our dining room was not heated, we chose to eat our meal huddled next to the stove. I remember thinking that the heat felt good on my face, but my back was ice cold.

About fifteen minutes later, my stomach was satisfied and I had become almost thawed. Mother and I played a quick game of Rummy while Dad caught up on the latest news from WSM Radio in Nashville. He would always finish the evening by listening to the area news, then the national news on the NBC Network at 6:00 p.m. Mother and I took our cue for bed when the network announcer came on with, "This is NBC News, I'm Morgan Beaty."

My bedroom was next to the dining room, and just like it, there was no heat. "Come on, son, and I'll tuck you in," Mother announced. I obeyed her request, but wasn't anxious to leave my warm spot next to the wood heater.

To You, My Grandchildren

Mother assured me that I would have pleasant dreams. That was fine, I thought, but would I stay warm? "I'll put some extra quilts on your bed," Mother assured. "You'll be all right," she said while covering me completely except for a small opening for my nose.

Almost as soon as she left the room, I was out like a light, nestled under a heavy layer of quilts. Later, I began to wake and wondered if morning had come already.

The moonlight reflected from my clock next to the bed. If I could just raise my head a little, I thought, then I'd be able to see the hands of time. It was 8:00 p.m. I remember thinking that I had been in bed half the night instead of only two hours.

If I could snuggle back down under the cover, turn over to my other side, then I could finish the night. What's this? Turning over while under the cover was never this difficult before. I remembered that I had never been covered with that many quilts on my bed. I tried turning, but again, I had the same difficulty.

A light went on in my head. I got the message. Slowly, with all my strength, I struggled and pushed the cover off my face and side. The air was cold. Quickly I turned to my other side and retrieved the cover. That was a job. I almost worked up a sweat. No time to think about it further. I quickly went back to sleep, dreading another morning at the barn.

Sure enough, 3:30 a.m. came quickly. Dad did his usual bit. "Son, it's time for us to make it to the barn."

"Okay, but will you help me out of this bed," I pleaded, knowing my difficulty earlier in the night with the quilts. When I returned to the house following my barn chores, I curiously counted the quilts covering my bed. There were only fourteen. I had sworn that there were at least a hundred.

To You, My Grandchildren

On Rain, Water, and Baths

For the last thirty minutes, I have been listening to the rain. The constant rhythm evokes a peaceful feeling. Being reared on a farm helps me appreciate the gentle rain that brings life and nourishment to our earth. When I was younger, the rain was often therapy when my tired, aching muscles needed solace from the day's work. Listening to the rain on our tin roof was better than a sleeping pill.

I remember as a boy the responsibility of helping with our dairy cows. The only milking machines then were my father and I. We could feed and milk by hand about thirty cows in two hours flat.

One particular aggravation with the job came on rainy days. The cows were herded into the barn, all dripping wet. You can imagine where most of the water fell when I was next to my benefactress gently squeezing the precious liquid from her.

The real test of my patience came when she decided to swish her rain-soaked tail. Without warning, it would come crashing against my face, leaving a sharp pain and a question in my mind about where her switch had been previously. It was part of doing the job, just like some of the unpleasant things in today's work world.

The rain tonight also reminds me of a more positive experience: bathing outdoors. We were spared the convenience of running water and indoor plumbing, so the rain signaled a perfect time to catch a shower. When Mother gave the assurance that it was safe outside, meaning free of lightning, I would don my swimming trunks, grab a bar of soap and go lickety-split through the house to the yard.

Although I could not adjust the water temperature, it didn't matter. I either stood in one spot or ran around in circles, being rejuvenated from head to toe. I always felt squeaky clean following those baths. The cleansing seemed to go deeper than my skin, touching the core of my spirit.

While reminiscing about my childhood and taking a bath, I'm reminded about taking a cold shower under a large waterfall located a few miles from our farm. Our home had no indoor plumbing and the waterfall was my surest method of getting an invigorating shower after a hot, tiring day on the farm.

The biggest problem, however, was that it took me about thirty minutes to walk from our house to the waterfall. It was nestled in a large hollow surrounded by steep hillsides. I remember the waterfall as being majestic because of its height.

To get under it required some ingenuity on my part. I had to wind around a maze of rocks and slowly descend about 150 feet to the bottom of the fall. I was usually soaked in perspiration when my feet were ready to step under the powerful spray.

I could have stayed under the water for hours although it was icy cold and hit hard against my skin. Those moments of pleasure erased the inconvenience of getting there. I am also reminded that we walk a mile only after taking the first step.

To You, My Grandchildren

The Peddler

While reading my newspaper tonight, I discovered humor in some advertisements by area merchants. They certainly are attention getting.

I read such lines as, "Check our everyday low prices." "I invite you to see the difference." "Get an extra 50% off." "You can double your coupons everyday." "There is never a dull moment here."

Part of the humor I found in those advertisements was the comparison between shopping today and what I experienced during my youth. My parents, just like parents today, wanted to cash in on the best buys of the week. However, in 1954 our options were limited to Underhill's Rolling Store, or what I called "the peddling truck." Our peddler, as we called him, actually provided a general store on wheels. He was our main source for groceries.

Talk about service! The peddler drove up to our front door. Our peddler became a memory in 1960 when "progress" replaced him with supermarkets and modern means of transportation.

I am now smiling as I try to imagine the peddling truck rolling down the road with advertisements tacked on the side of the vehicle: Quality costs less. There is never a dull moment here.

What if the peddler had a price scanner like those used in today's supermarkets? It sure would have been easier for him than scribbling down each item's price on a brown paper sack. My mother always double-checked the peddler's figures, like any good price-conscious shopper should. Some supermarkets today advertise that if their scanner makes a mistake, the item is given to you at no cost. Back in the 1950s, our peddler would simply apologize for a mistake, make the correction, and sometimes throw in a free stick of peppermint candy to sweeten the inconvenience.

I wonder what a supermarket clerk would do today if offered a fat chicken as trade for a package of bologna? That is what we sometimes did back in the 50's. The peddler also had a limited deli department, offering a choice of either crackers and cheese or crackers and bologna.

The old peddling truck had a unique aroma. It smelled of oil and grease from the truck engine, of the odor from the chicken coops, of livestock feed mingled with the sweet smell of molasses, and of the dust that covered the peddling truck from top to bottom.

To You, My Grandchildren

The roads through New Home and Cross Roads communities were not paved back then, so the dirty peddling truck became a source of entertainment for us kids. In the dirt on the truck we would etch our names and messages such as "Wash me," "Smile," and "It's a great life."

The peddler was a man of travel moving from one small community to the next. He was our newsman and weather prognosticator. I remember him also telling jokes, all acceptable in mixed company. Sometimes while shopping now, I barely get a "thank you" from a store clerk.

The peddler had good insight into human relations. Many times we did not have enough money to pay for our groceries. His response was, "Ah, you can pay me next week or at the end of the month. I'll be back to see you."

Try asking a supermarket clerk to let you pay your bill next week.

To You, My Grandchildren

Pat

Today was a beautiful day filled with plenty of sunshine and pleasant temperatures. I appreciate the sunshine, but I also remember that each day is a special gift no matter the weather. One of my favorite sayings puts the weather and life in good perspective: The sun always shines; it depends on my attitude as to whether I see it. Keeping a positive attitude is vital to maintaining a proper altitude.

When I was a youngster working on our farm, there were days when I prayed for rain, not because we necessarily needed precipitation, but because rain meant not having to work in the fields. Of course the jobs still had to be completed even if they were delayed by a few days.

We grew large fields of tobacco and strawberries. Those rows must have been ten miles long. At least they were in my mind. It was amazing how quickly time passed once I began working. Before long, the job was finished. How did I do that, I would always wonder.

Dad gave Pat and me the responsibility of cultivating the crops. We worked the soil and spent many long days and hot summers together. We became good friends.

Sometimes I questioned Pat's loyalty, especially when I thought he wasn't pulling his share of the load. I rebuffed him by raising my voice in disapproval. That always made Pat nervous. I could tell because his work quality decreased. It later occurred to me that Pat tried harder to do a good job when my words were encouraging rather than demanding. Isn't that true in almost every situation?

Pat and I shared many conversations. I did the talking while he did the listening. He heard about all my dreams, my hurts and even my inhibitions as a bashful kid who wanted to discover where I belonged in life. Pat just nodded his head as he continued to work. I think he understood me although Pat was a mule.

To You, My Grandchildren

Basketball at Cross Roads

I marvel at the ability of young people today who play the game of basketball. They amaze me by dribbling the ball between their legs or behind their backs.

My own sports career in the 1950's at Cross Roads Elementary was average at best. However, Cross Roads had a tradition of producing some pretty competitive basketball teams.

I remember having to practice on the school's outside court. Back then, only three schools in DeKalb County had gymnasiums: Smithville, Liberty, and Alexandria. Cross Roads was considered a country school, meaning outside playground facilities and outside restrooms. Some of the other country schools included Blue Springs, Belk, Midway, Peeled Chestnut, New View and Pea Ridge.

Larry Stanley, my best friend, and I practiced basketball almost year round no matter what the weather. Even with freezing temperatures outside, we could usually be found during recess shooting basketballs until our hands were almost numb from the cold. I guess we believed in the theory of "No Pain, No Gain."

After practice, we washed our dirty hands in cold water from an outside faucet because there was no hot water available. I wonder how many students today would practice basketball under those conditions.

While musing tonight, I recall the thrill of making the team and earning a suit. That seemed to erase the sacrifices I may have made in sharpening my basketball skills. Our school colors were simply black and white. After all, Cross Roads was just an average country school.

Remembering Larry Stanley tonight also reminded me of my neglect of a once exemplary friendship. He and I were almost inseparable through elementary school and during our four years at DeKalb County High. We even fought for each other on a few occasions. I was his best man and he was mine at our first marriages. I should have made an extra effort to stay in touch with him over the years since school.

To You, My Grandchildren

Christmas Lessons

Any person can usually list a number of disappointments that has occurred in his life. Typically most adults mention career opportunities that were missed, business deals that fell through, personal relationships that broke apart, and their shortcomings.

A young person's perspective on life usually produces a different response. I remember experiencing many disappointments as a youngster. My first major disappointment came a week before Christmas in 1955. I was excited about the approaching "big" day and the possibility of what Santa Claus might bring me.

The year before had been slightly disappointing. I was convinced beyond a doubt that Santa would place a bright green bicycle under my Christmas tree. After all, I had done my part by being good in order to gain Santa's favor. Instead, he left a neatly-wrapped package containing two handkerchiefs and a shirt. I later told my friends that Santa brought me "clothes" for Christmas. To a seven-year-old, that sounded more appropriate than telling the truth.

Somehow, I just knew this next Christmas was going to be different. I was now eight and still believed in Santa's magic.

At the rear of our small weatherboard house stood a storage building, or what we called the "smoke house." Actually, our smoke house was no more than an 8 x 12 foot frame structure that was usually cluttered with farming tools or canning jars. It was also my playhouse.

The week before Christmas of 1955 found me in the smoke house playing my usual childhood games. The smoke house often became my radio station where I announced the top hits of the day. The smoke house could become anything I imagined, an airplane, an automobile, or anything else my young mind could conceive.

On this particular day, I spotted a tarpaulin that looked out of place covering one corner of the smoke house. I wondered what it was doing there. Maybe Dad had covered some feed or fertilizer to keep it dry, I thought. Oh well, it is not important, I concluded. I had other things to think about.

But there was almost a magnetic attraction that kept pulling me back to the tarpaulin. What was it that seemed so strange, so mysterious?

To You, My Grandchildren

My curiosity became overpowering. I had to look under that covering. Slowly I raised the tarp, took one look, froze in place for at least five minutes, and then went storming out of the smoke house. Part of me was crying with happiness. Another part was filled with anger and disbelief.

Under the tarpaulin was my bicycle, the answer to my Christmas prayer. But if that is my bicycle, I thought, can there be a Santa Claus? I had discovered the truth and the truth hurt. I never shared that disappointment with anyone until after I had become an adult.

To You, My Grandchildren

Easter

Today is Easter. As a Christian, this is a special day, a day that symbolizes the hope that every believer has through Jesus Christ. My belief is that Jesus became the victor over sin and death when He died and rose to new life almost two-thousand years ago. His sacrifice and my faith in Him give assurance of eternal life with God. I could never explain it. In fact, a person could lose his mind trying, but we would lose our souls if we reject it.

When I was a youngster, Easter was a special day to visit relatives and participate in a family Easter egg hunt to see who could find the most eggs. My fondest memories of Easter as a child, however, were the years when I attended Cross Roads Elementary School. Easter egg hunts were major productions back then. Each student was required to bring his or her own hard-boiled chicken eggs to school. We were given time to dye the eggs and paint them however our imagination inspired. Then all eggs were collected in a large basket for the big hunt. Afterward, we were allowed to eat the reward of our hard work, which always left me suspicious of whose eggs I had found and of their quality.

In 1958, I was ten years old and in the fifth grade, my first year to be in the Big Room. The school-sponsored Easter egg hunts had been fun every year to that point, but I was getting frustrated. The golden egg – or top prize – had always been found by someone other than me. I would watch each year as the lucky winner was rewarded with a beautiful Easter basket filled with chocolate bunnies and candy eggs. The second-prize was a smaller basket for the student who found the most eggs. That, too, had eluded me because of the faster-running boys and girls.

I figured that this Easter would be just like the rest, but maybe there was still hope for me. In desperation, I prayed, "Lord, please help me this year. Please let me find the golden egg. To show you, Lord, that I'm not selfish, just let me find one other egg to go along with the golden egg. Remember, Lord, if I find only two eggs, I'll be happy."

Whether by divine intervention or merely by coincidence, my prayer was answered. That was my happiest Easter at Cross Roads School, an event that never repeated itself. I wonder how many prayers are directed to God in that manner. I suspect that even as

To You, My Grandchildren

an adult, I may be guilty of praying for my desires rather than see-ing others' needs.

To You, My Grandchildren

Valentine's Day

As far back as I can remember, Valentine's Day has always been extra special. To me, every day is special because it affords another experience in living. Each day is an opportunity to learn something new. Valentine's Day, however, reminds me to be thankful for the people who are near and dear to my heart.

Valentine's Day has a totally different meaning for me now compared to forty years ago. My first recollection goes back to preschool age. I remember February 14 as the day to exchange valentines with Mack and JoAnn Ervin, an uncle and aunt slightly older than me. We were neighbors and played together every day. Our relationship was so close I could have been their brother. They also became my guardians when I first entered Cross Roads School at age five.

My fondest memories of Valentine's Day were made at Cross Roads. I then thought the proof of a person's acceptance was the number of valentines he collected. Every year, I was faithful in giving one to each of my classmates and then expanded the list to include every other person in the room. Our school had only two-rooms: the Little Room, for grades one through four, and the Big Room, for grades five through eight.

Although I never admitted it, the truth was that I gave a valentine hoping to get one in return. About a week before Valentine's Day, I became a pretty good politician, speaking to everyone, offering someone my place in the lunch line, and even agreeing to help with their homework. It is easy to be nice when you expect something in return.

I guess life as an adult is about the same. Most of us want to be accepted and have others know our name. We are sometimes motivated to do things for others just so they will accept us.

The recent years have taught me the importance of doing unto others without a motive of receiving. However, it appears that I get more when I give more.

A successful businessman and philanthropist once said that everyone needs a magnificent obsession to motivate them to greater accomplishment. I have adopted this as my own Magnificent Obsession: The desire to make the world a better place to live. Like many others, I suppose, having fame and a life

To You, My Grandchildren

of ease were once what I viewed as success. Being from a humble background taught me to appreciate the things I receive; however, it also caused me as a young person to believe that only popularity and material possessions were the measure of a man. Age has hopefully brought me wisdom and a wiser perspective on the things that matter most in life.

Today has been a good Valentine's Day. It has helped me remember the "real" things in life that are truly valuable. On this Valentine's Day I am making a renewed commitment to my Magnificent Obsession: Make this world a better place to live.

To You, My Grandchildren

Incident at Center Hill Lake

I enjoy reminding people that every day is a holiday. When they question what I mean by a holiday, I'm quick to respond, "Well, if you don't believe that every day is a holiday, try doing without one sometime." My purpose is to get the listener to think about the value of every precious day, not to dazzle them with my philosophical wit.

Today I was reminded of this saying while I was looking out the window at the beautiful blue water of a nearby lake. The view has a real calming effect on me, putting my mind in neutral and keeping me from thinking about anything in particular.

Suddenly, a giant television screen flashed on in my mind. I imagined a news reporter on the scene describing a near tragedy. "On a day almost like this one fifty years ago," he announces, "a young lad nearly four years old was pulled from the water at Center Hill Lake near Smithville, Tennessee." He points to a spot in the lake where a fishing boat is moored by a long rope about thirty feet from the water's edge. "According to information I have been given," the reporter continues, "a woman on the scene abandoned all regard for her own safety and snatched a young boy from the mouth of this blue abyss." He is pointing at what appears to be an extremely deep cavity in the otherwise shallow portion of Center Hill Lake. "I am sure that lady believes today is a special day for both her and the boy."

I remember the whole story. The boy had pulled on the rope, thinking naively that he could somehow manage to get the boat close enough to jump in it. Quickly, he looked around to see where all the others had gone. Several families had taken this particularly pretty afternoon to share a picnic. The men had walked further down the shore to try their luck at fishing. The women and other children were busy boxing up the leftover fried chicken and other remnants of a delicious meal outdoors. No one was looking, so the boy made his move for the boat. Things didn't go according to his plans, and he suddenly became overbalanced, falling head first into the water. Not knowing how to swim, he panicked, yelling at the top of his lungs. The first person in the water after him was the lady, the same one the reporter had spoken to. She stretched out her hand. The boy latched on. She pulled him into her arms and stepped quickly toward dry land. The boy had fallen into water that was nearly over his head, but only inches away was the abyss described by the reporter.

Fifty years is a long time, but I still remember the most aggravating and embarrassing part of the whole episode. The lady was my mother. Obviously, the boy was me. Since I had no other dry clothes with me that day, Mother pinned a diaper on me. I was hopping mad. How could anyone have the audacity to put a diaper on a boy almost four years old? I hid in the backseat of our neighbor's car for the remainder of the afternoon while my clothes dried in the sun.

Yes, I believe today is a holiday.

First Smoke

I smoked my first cigarette in 1952. Really, I should admit that it was an attempt to smoke a "roll your own" Country Gentleman.

My dad was real proficient at taking a small, thin sheet of paper with his fingers and rolling a portion of the Country Gentleman tobacco into a near-perfect cigarette. After watching Dad perform his marvelous feat of dexterity so many times, I reasoned that I could sit right down and do the same thing.

Dad had warned me with unquestioning resolve that I should always do as he said, not as he did, when considering any vices in life. "Don't ever let me catch you using tobacco," he plainly advised, "and that goes for either smoking or chewing." I knew there was no compromise in what he said, although he smoked several cigarettes daily.

Have you ever noticed how many of us bend things to fit our particular situation? I knew better than to go against my father's rules, but I wanted to try my skill at rolling a cigarette and puffing smoke like my dad. After all, he had said, and I remembered every word, "Don't let me catch you using tobacco." Did that mean it was all right as long as I didn't get caught? I heard what I wanted to hear and decided on my course of action.

One day while Dad and Mother were away from the house at work, I gingerly opened Dad's large box of Country Gentleman tobacco, removed one of the small bags, and quickly hid it inside my shirt. I glanced around the room thinking I heard a noise. Was that Mother and Dad returning unexpectedly? I waited for a few moments without moving. It was only my imagination; I remembered that they wouldn't be home until later in the day. I then made a beeline out the back door through the yard and raced nearly two hundred yards to a small creek that meandered near our house. Crouching behind a tree, my moment of truth had arrived.

Let me think how Dad did it, I conspired to myself. First, take the paper in one hand; and then with the other hand, measure out the right portion of tobacco for the cigarette. Everything proceeded as planned until it was time to make the roll.

My first attempt was not a pretty sight. The cigarette was too fat in the middle. The paper began to tear while I was struggling to make it stick together after moistening the strange looking wad

31

with my tongue.

Next came the challenge of lighting what was supposed to be a cigarette. Finally, I got a match struck. I inhaled deeply, trying to get the cigarette lit. I pulled the smoke deeply into my throat and lungs. I almost lost my breath and began coughing while panic gripped my chest.

This had never happened to Dad. Where did I go wrong? Slowly, the blood returned to my face, but I didn't feel so good. What should I do next? I must destroy the evidence, but where?

There was a decayed spot in a large tree near the creek. Maybe I could hide the tobacco there. It'll never be found, I thought.

The mission was accomplished, but how would I explain the feeling of nausea? Maybe Mother and Dad would accept the explanation that I simply got too hot while playing and became sick.

Later, after they had returned, Dad appeared to be a little suspicious. Maybe it was my guilt showing through. "Son, have you been in my Country Gentleman tobacco?" he quizzed.

"What do you mean, Dad?" I responded. "You always said to never let you catch me using tobacco. You don't see me smoking or anything, do you?"

"I had six sacks of tobacco in that box this morning. Now, there are only five. What do you suppose happened to it?" he asked.

I couldn't stand the pressure any longer. I blurted out the whole truth while reminding Dad that he really did say for me never to let him catch me using tobacco. "You didn't see me using tobacco," I pleaded while imagining what was about to happen next.

My expectation came true. He removed his leather belt, looked me directly in the eyes, and said softly with a sound of pain in his voice, "This is going to hurt me more than it does you; but you must always listen to what I say and not just listen to what you want to hear."

I couldn't understand then how my whipping hurt him more than it did me. Now that I have children and grandchildren of my own, I fully understand what he meant.

To You, My Grandchildren

Starting High School

I recall hearing someone say, "Dwell on the reward of success, not on the penalty of failure." Little did I know at age thirteen what that principle means, but apparently I began to practice it.

I had completed eighth grade at Cross Roads School, spent the summer working on our farm, and was now ready for the big world of high school at Pure Fountain in Smithville, Tennessee.

All through the summer while anticipating my first year at Pure Fountain, I wondered what it would be like going to school in a two-story building with hundreds of students. I had heard that in high school boys and girls even held hands while walking in the halls. I guess that is how it is when you grow up and begin to have girlfriends and dates, I thought. It was scary enough to think about attending high school, let alone having to consider the idea of having a girlfriend. I'll never fit into that system, I remember thinking.

Summer passed, and the first day of school arrived. Nervously, I took my regular morning bath with a washcloth and a pan of water. I bathed in the privacy of my bedroom with the washcloth and pan of water. I remember putting on extra Wild Root Cream Oil to slick my hair into place. I was always embarrassed about having curly hair and tried to straighten it by applying the greasy hair oil.

The first day at high school was horrible. First, there was an assembly of all the students in the auditorium. The principal, Mr. Walter Fowler, welcomed us and challenged everyone to become good students and to do our best in class. When his speech was over, we were told to visit the rooms where our teachers were standing by to enroll us in their classes. I'll never learn my way around this large, two-story building, I thought. Too shy to ask questions, I just followed the crowd down the hall and luckily spotted the room that was marked "Miss Jodie Conger—Freshman Arithmetic." That was to be my first subject. I remember one person in particular that day. He was Paul Keith, who was probably a junior but was signing up for freshman arithmetic. I also remember Miss Jodie reminding Paul that if he didn't conform to the rules of her room, he would not be welcome again. He replied that he was going to be an exemplary student, although those were not the words he used.

I made it through that first day, but I still don't know how. On returning home, I announced to my mother that high school was not for me. "Mother, I'll do anything," I pleaded. "Just let me quit school. I'll work at the shirt factory. I'll work in the fields. I'll go into the army. I'll do anything if you'll just let me quit school."

Mother looked stunned. Her face dropped. "Neither your father nor I had an opportunity to attend high school," she said softly. "We want you to have a better life than we have had. You need to get an education and be somebody. You have always talked about being a radio announcer. You'll never have that opportunity without an education."

She showed her wisdom when she said, "I'll tell you what. Try it one more day; and if you still feel the same way, we'll let you quit school." This same scene went on for about two weeks. Each day she insisted, "Please try school one more day to make sure you still want to quit."

It happened. I slowly became accustomed to the high school environment. I never mentioned quitting high school again. Although I didn't understand it back then, there was one principle that carried me for the next four years: If you concentrate or dwell on the reward of success and not the penalty of failure and frustration, you will succeed. I wanted to become a radio announcer; after all, I had dreamed about it for six years. By holding the reward of that success in my mind, not the penalty of failure, I had the resolve to find extra strength and courage. I graduated from DeKalb County High School in 1965, the first in my family to graduate.

To You, My Grandchildren

First Car

Small boys think about bicycles. Larger boys think about cars. I remember dreaming about owning my first automobile. My thoughts were filled with images of something sporty like a 1956 Ford or 1957 Chevrolet, complete with four-in-the-floor transmission, fancy chrome, pin striping, and bucket seats.

In 1965, I was seventeen years old and ready to discover my dream car. I had saved $1,000 and was eager to check all the options available. Since I believed back then that all car dealers were silver-tongued and ready to take me for a ride, I asked my father to help me make a deal.

He agreed to check around and see what was available. "I'll stop by some car lots tomorrow after taking our milk to the Kraft plant in Alexandria," he offered. I was ready to buy a car at that moment, but conceded that another day wouldn't make a difference.

Dad was briefed thoroughly on what to look for in selecting my first car. I described it to a "T." Sure enough, Dad came through the next day. "Son, I found just what you need while looking over the cars at Center Hill Chrysler this morning," he announced.

"Please tell me more," I encouraged him while visions of fast cars with fancy gadgets flashed through my mind.

"Well, you'll just have to see it to appreciate it," he remarked. "It's a 1963 model, sporty looking, white with red interior, bucket seats and has a great sounding radio." I could hardly wait to see and test drive it.

Upon arriving at Center Hill Chrysler, I quickly glanced down the rows and rows of new and used cars. "Where is it, Dad?" I asked. "Show me, hurry."

Ernest Crook, the owner, appeared and motioned for us to come inside. "I've got the boys cleaning up the car. You all come on in, and I'll make you a real deal." His price sounded reasonable. He pointed out that the car had only been used two years, had 53,000 actual miles, and could be counted on for at least 100,000 with no major problems. This is all good, I thought, but just show me the car.

Next, he led us into the dealership's garage and announced,

To You, My Grandchildren

"Here is the perfect car for you, young man." I didn't see anything with tail fins or a fancy grill. "This is it," he said, proudly gesturing with his hands.

I was almost speechless. Before my eyes was what was to be my first car. Like Dad had promised, it was white, red interior, bucket seats, good radio, but I didn't see the four-in-the-floor gear stick.

"How do I change gears?" I asked while explaining that I expected a car with manual transmission.

"Look here," Mr. Crook pointed out. "This car has a push button system. You could say it has three on the dash, first, second and drive."

Needless to say, a 1963 Plymouth Valiant was not what I expected as my first car, especially with the three-on-the-dash. It became a great little car for me, however, one that provided many miles of dependable transportation.

To You, My Grandchildren

Firsts in Life

Some friends of mine have become celebrities on national television. The City Cafe in Murfreesboro was transformed this morning into a remote studio for *Adam Smith's Money World*, a PBS syndicated series broadcast by 250 television stations in America and also seen in Singapore and Russia.

I was proud to see Andrea Loughry, Mike Pirtle, John Bragg, Ted LaRoche, and Mike Broll respond calmly and confidently to questions from Jerry Goodman, the host and editor-in-chief for *Money World*. The show's focus was on national issues like the war in Iraq, the recession, and education rather than a promotion for Murfreesboro. However, I think the guests did a splendid job of representing the Heart of Tennessee.

While watching the television taping, I assumed that today's experience was a "first" for each of my friends. John Bragg may be an exception because of his national leadership roles through state government. Witnessing their first appearance on national television caused me to muse over some of the "firsts" in my life.

First Time to Drive: I was eight years old and too small to reach the accelerator with my foot. Dad allowed me to sit in his lap, steer the wheel, and maneuver the gear stick from the column of the pick-up while he pressed the gas pedal.

First Kiss: I was seventeen in 1965 and had just graduated from DeKalb County High School. Keep in mind that I had never dated a girl. My friend, Jerry Kirby, whom I believed back then was every woman's dream of an ideal man, proposed we go riding in his white 1959 Thunderbird. I had never ridden in a Thunderbird and was a little frightened with his suggestion that we "check out some chicks." I did have a few girls who chased me while in high school; but because I was so shy, they never caught me. I agreed to go along with his plan, but secretly hoped that "the chicks" would not be available for the ride. As fate would have it, Nancy and Brenda were parked at the Sunrise Grill, a popular hangout in Smithville.

Jerry did all the talking. I smiled and blushed as they got into the car with us. Nancy and Jerry were nestled in the front seat. Brenda and I were in the back.

The combination of winding country roads, music on the

37

To You, My Grandchildren

radio, and action from the front seat set the stage for my destiny. Brenda must have foreseen the future. She began moving toward my side of the car. What should I do next? I put my right arm around her shoulder and gently pulled her closer. There was no resistance. Now what should I do? I looked into her eyes and quickly glanced at her lips. Brenda has done this before, I thought. My heart almost pounded out of my chest. Half-frozen with fear, I closed my eyes and puckered my lips. What should I do next? Nothing, because Brenda took the lead and turned that "first" kiss into a memorable experience.

First Job: My first real experience on the radio was disastrous. The program director had coached me thoroughly on what was expected during my first radio program. After the first record was over, I was to welcome the listeners, give a time and temperature check, and introduce the second record of the hour. That sounded easy enough, but I was still scared. The station identification was announced by the retiring DJ. He flipped the switch, and my first song began playing. Three minutes of music were consumed in three seconds, or so it seemed. Now it was my turn on the air. I cleared my throat. The parts seemed to work. The music began fading. I opened my mouth but nothing came out. A cardinal sin in broadcasting is to have "dead air" or total silence. In fact, I was a sinner in the highest degree because there were at least sixty seconds of dead air. Panic gripped me. What should I do? Play another record and catch my breath were all I could think of doing.

When the second record finished playing, I cautiously said my spiel and began living my dream for the next twenty-one years.

Chapter 5:

Punches on Attitude

To be happy, you must want to be happy.

•

Imagine the best. Believe the best.

•

Your thoughts determine your attitude and your attitude determines your success.

•

Express your positive attitude in words and actions.

•

Remain optimistic by associating with positive, happy people.

•

Ability will put you on top but character will keep you there.

•

I am healthy. I am happy. By the grace of God, I am getting better and better right now.

•

Recognize, relate and assimilate positive principles of life.

•

Every negative has a positive. Find it.

•

Keep your mind on what you want in life.

•

We become what we think about.

•

Open your mind. Stimulate new thinking.

•

Prove your worth.

•

There is an island of opportunity in the middle of every difficulty.

To You, My Grandchildren

Real leaders are ordinary people
with extraordinary determination.

•

The control center of your life is your attitude.

•

You are never fully dressed without a smile.

•

A different world cannot be built by indifferent people.

•

Feed your faith, and your doubts will starve to death.

•

Maintain a spirit of open-mindedness.

•

Success can be achieved through a positive mental attitude.

•

Be the master of your emotions.

•

As is your confidence, so is your capacity.

•

You have unlimited potential. Most limits are self-imposed.

•

Be open to change. It is the most constant thing in life.

•

Your attitude gives you the power to control your future.

•

You are a wonderful creation. Act as if you believe it.

•

To be taken seriously,
people must perceive that you are believable.

•

Many people go through life as if they are in some kind of stupor.
Be alert. Think, plan and take action.

•

Daily assimilate positive thoughts into positive actions.

•

The right attitude puts adventure, romance and
excitement into each day.

•

Open the door to your future. Open your mind to the possibilities
before you.

To You, My Grandchildren

Your true age is determined by your attitude rather than by the years you have lived.

•

You must believe in your worth.

•

Put your mind at ease. Think smart, but also think calmly.

•

Expect the best.

•

Your mind is like a garden. Seed it with positive thoughts.

•

According to your faith is what you will receive.

•

A positive attitude is a matter of habit.

•

Your attitude is more important than your aptitude.

•

Prayer changes things: me.

•

Courtesy makes everyone feel good.

•

Become genuinely interested in other people.

•

It's hard to see the picture when you're inside the frame.

•

A wise person realizes that sincerity is a strong force.

•

Now and then it's good to pause in your pursuit of happiness and just be happy.

•

Practice a calm, relaxed attitude toward the world and your life.

•

Real strength to face life is inside you.

•

When you look at other people, look for the good. You'll be surprised at what you find.

•

Let's accept each other as we are, only then will we discover each other.

To You, My Grandchildren

Being poor is a frame of mind. We can be broke,
but we never have to be poor.

•

Happiness is not found in outside circumstances but inside yourself.

•

We can't purchase enough insurance to cover all possible problems,
but we can have a positive attitude to provide assurance.

•

When we believe the best will happen and it doesn't,
we have still lost nothing.

•

If you feel you have no faults, that makes at least one.

•

There is a power in you, and no one but you knows what you can do.

•

A cheerful attitude is like a good medicine to those
around you.

•

Positiveness produces more positiveness.

•

Anyone who attempts to do anything positively
will be criticized. Do it anyway!

•

Think and talk good health,
never about what is wrong with you.

•

Be open-minded toward all people.

•

Attitude is a little thing that makes a big difference.

•

Transform your life by using powerful, positive ideas.

Chapter 6: Radio Days

Becoming a DJ

I suppose everyone I've met has left their mark on my life. I'm reminded of Ronnie and Donnie Young, as well as Joe, Roy, James, Billy, and Kenneth Harris. They were almost like brothers to me when we were children, rather than cousins.

Douglas Braswell, another cousin, was one of my special friends and regular playmates. Douglas was my most loyal supporter while I dreamed of becoming a radio broadcaster.

He drove me to WJLE Radio in Smithville on the memorable Saturday afternoon in 1965 when I appeared as a winner in the station's "DJ For A Day" contest. I have since wondered how many other people, if any, entered the competition by mailing in their reasons for wanting to be a guest DJ at the radio station. That afternoon set the stage for my radio career.

Jack Baker was host of the radio show and originator of the contest. Tony Glenn Rast, WJLE manager, came by the station to offer me his congratulations. His first comments were an answer to a prayer held in my heart for almost ten years: to be a radio announcer.

"You are pretty good at reading the news," Tony remarked. I should be, I thought. After all, I had been practicing since I was seven years old.

"If you'll get a license, I'll use you some part-time," Tony promised. How do I get a license was my question to him. "You take a test," he answered. I never knew a person had to be tested in order to talk on the radio.

My questions were all amusing to Tony. "Do I have to be a certain height, weight, or...?" I queried.

"You simply answer questions about radio rules and regulations," Tony responded. "You can go to Atlanta, Georgia, for the

43

testing procedure."

Getting to Atlanta sounded simple, but for a timid seventeen-year-old kid who had never been outside Middle Tennessee, that was almost like "Mission Impossible."

To You, My Grandchildren

Getting My Broadcaster's License

My fascination with broadcasting began when I started attending the annual Warren County Fair in McMinnville. I was seven years old at the time.

Both McMinnville radio stations, WBMC and WMMT (now WAKI), had remote studios at the fairgrounds during the week-long event. I would literally stand for hours watching the DJs play records, read the news and interview fairgoers.

If only I could talk like they talk, I wished. Keep in mind that I was probably the most introverted child who ever lived; at least that is how I felt about myself. This complex evolved from my belief that everyone had more money, better looks, and more talent than me.

For the next ten years, however, I worked regularly at my mythical radio station, charming the audience with my catchy adlibs and clever record introductions, and occasionally taking time to sign a few autographs.

I remember smiling at the imaginary microphone while introducing the shook snook Sam Cook, Elvis the Pelvis, the killer Jerry Lee Lewis, and the amazing Little Richard. My make-believe studio included a record turntable that was actually Mother's wooden dresser. My microphone was her large hairbrush. I simply pantomimed the radio announcers and pretended to push all the right buttons while the radio played in the background.

My big break came in 1965 when I won WJLE's "DJ For A Day" contest. Following the advise of Tony Glenn Rast, I became determined to get a broadcasting license no matter what would be required of me, even going to Atlanta.

My father could not be counted on to drive me there because of his commitment to the farm, milking, feeding, and all the other chores. The only option I knew was to catch a Trailways bus from Smithville and head south.

I remember the fare was $29 round trip. It should be a breeze, I thought. I will just get on the bus Monday afternoon at 3:15, arrive in Atlanta at 11:20 p.m., and then relax until the Federal Communications Commission office opens at 8:00 a.m. Tuesday morning.

One thing I failed to notice about my ticket was a 30 minute holdover in Chattanooga. That was to become an experience I will forever remember.

I was scared to leave my seat in the Chattanooga bus station, afraid that the Atlanta bound coach would depart without me. "Bus now departing for points south....Dalton, Atl...," the voice on the intercom mumbled. I failed to understand what was said and was too shy to ask anyone. I thought that surely he would announce Atlanta soon and I'd be on my way.

One hour passed and I was still fastened to my seat. I kept thinking, that the Atlanta bus should be leaving soon. Another hour passed. I swallowed, gained a little confidence and walked to the counter. "Excuse me...please excuse me...I don't want to trouble you...but when will the bus leave for Atlanta?" I almost whispered.

"Son, that bus left two hours ago," the man responded. "I'm sorry." Almost in tears, my mind began to race at 100 miles per hour. It seemed like a million questions were dancing in my head. Here I was halfway around the world, and I didn't know a soul.

The man comforted me when he said, "I'm going to transfer your ticket to the Greyhound Company. They have a bus leaving at 11:00 for Atlanta. You only have to walk three blocks down one street and then two blocks down another." I could have died on the spot.

Timidly, I took the ticket and headed out the door. He told me to go three blocks down one street and then...I had forgotten the rest of his directions. "Lord, please help me," I quickly prayed. "Please, please don't let me down."

In almost an instant, a ragged-looking gentleman called out to me. I thought that maybe the Lord had sent him to rescue me. "Sir, can you tell me the correct way to the Greyhound bus station?" I stammered.

"Come with me," he summoned. While we walked, he told of his bout with hard luck and asked if I could spare some money so that he could get something to eat. I handed him a dollar. He accepted my gift, pointed to the Greyhound station, and then vanished almost as quickly as he had appeared. I still wonder if he was an angel sent to rescue me or if he was a panhandler working the streets.

46

Once in Atlanta, I spent the remainder of the night glued to a bench in the bus station. I remember hearing one record being played over and over on a jukebox, Ramsey Lewis' "The In Crowd."

Daylight found me still attached to the bench. What a night that had been. I remember thinking, I will never leave Smithville again. I stood, stretched, and then quickly rushed to the restroom to wash the sleep from my eyes and get composed for the test that was ahead.

Where is the FCC building? Which direction should I go? The best thing to do is to catch a taxi, I thought. I was in luck. One was parked in front of the bus station. I got inside the car and announced that my stop was the Merchandise Mart on Peachtree Street.

The driver laughed and pointed to a tall building, only a half block from where we were. "I'll drive you," he volunteered. He must have sensed how frightened I was.

The testing procedure took exactly one hour. I was confident that all my preparation had paid off, although I would not know the official results for two weeks. I returned to the bus station, waited until departure time, boarded the bus, and settled in for the return trip.

That moment was one of the happiest in my life. I felt secure again with my thoughts of home in Smithville.

To You, My Grandchildren

Early Days in Radio

The grass usually appears greener on the other side of the fence. Someone once said that the grass is just as hard to cut no matter which side of the fence you're on.

My dream as a starry-eyed kid was to get a job one day at WSM Radio in Nashville and earn a hundred dollars a week. I thought the "big time" was being able to earn that amount of money. In 1957, a hundred dollars sounded bigger to me than it does today.

WSM Radio came to my mind today while reminiscing about such programs as *Amos and Andy, The Lone Ranger, Roy Rogers and Dale Evans, Sergeant Preston of the Yukon,* and *Gunsmoke.* They were a staple of my weekly radio appetite when I was a youngster growing up in Smithville. Those popular programs also helped to fuel my dream of one day becoming a radio personality.

One of the highlights during my 21 years in broadcasting was getting to audition at WSM in 1973. Dave Overton, the program director, invited me to their studios on Knob Hill in Nashville after receiving a copy of my resume.

He took me on a tour through the station and later had me record some news copy and commercials. Dave thanked me and promised to keep the tape and resume on file. Getting to audition at WSM was almost as important to me as actually landing the job. I never again applied at WSM.

I later became convinced that small market radio was where I belonged. My mission statement, I believed, was more compatible with the role of a small market station than one in a larger city. My mission, you will recall, is to help make the world a better place, and to improve my mind and deepen my appreciation for life on a daily basis.

As a youngster, the fast-talking DJs appealed to me as celebrities. Once I was in broadcasting, however, my values changed because of such people as Franklin (Chick) Brown and Dr. W.E. Vanatta. They taught me the importance of community service and how the media can make a positive difference in a community.

I used my influence in radio to help raise money for Little League Baseball, the high school band, the football team, and for people who lost their belongings to disaster. I also remember helping a young man get life-saving medical attention after he was seriously injured in a traffic accident. He didn't have insurance, so we raised enough money to get him admitted to Vanderbilt Hospital in Nashville, a move which saved his life. In my opinion, that is how a small market radio station can be an integral part of a community.

My first full-time job in radio was in 1965 at WJLE Radio in Smithville, where I earned $50 a week. Even then, I still thought $100 a week in income was the ultimate. My second job really advanced me further up the ladder of success.

Chick Brown of WBMC enticed me to join his station in McMinnville in 1966 with an offer of $80 weekly. I then climbed to what I perceived to be the top rung on the ladder in 1970 when WJLE made me an offer to return to Smithville. Their bid was more money than I had ever seen at one time: a cool $125 a week. I could hardly believe what was happening in my career: only five years in the industry, and I had made it to the top.

Reality soon woke me from my euphoria when I discovered that even $125 a week didn't go far enough when supporting a wife, a young son and paying for our first home. The mortgage payment alone was $70 a month.

My conclusion is that everything is relative to where a person is in life. I also believe that a person can usually find what he or she is looking for.

To You, My Grandchildren

Sleeping In

I recently was forced to stay in bed during the weekend because of a bout with the "bug." The time allowed me to reminisce about one particular weekend when I was seventeen years old.

To put the story in proper perspective, I must explain that part of my responsibility growing up on a farm was to perform certain chores at the barn. This required dedication, although I confess that mine was externally rather than internally motivated.

Each morning at 3:30 a.m., I was awakened with the same message that was repeated 365 days a year. "Son, it's time for us to get it," Dad encouraged while I was resting so peacefully beneath the covers.

He never had to call me twice. I knew better because I had survived two of his best chastisements. A third would never be necessary.

Almost ten years of this routine had given me some proper training on how to wake quickly and get prepared for a new day. Maybe that is one of the reasons why I am an early morning person now. The early morning is truly a great time to put the day in perspective and to get organized.

Now getting back to where my story began. I had dreamed almost every day during those years on the farm about how life would be when I got my first "real" job. Then I could abandon this early morning schedule and learn to "sleep in," maybe even learn to sleep until six or seven o'clock each morning.

WJLE Radio was now providing me with a paycheck, modest though it was. I was making $1.25 per hour. However, I still owned two cows and had a pretty good "nest egg" from selling milk and from hiring myself out to neighbors who needed my brawn more than my brain.

It was Sunday, and being gainfully employed in public work, I decided to begin the new adventure of sleeping later. I had forgotten something important. I didn't bother to tell my dad.

"Son, it's time for us to get it," the familiar voice reminded. My bubble came crashing down. I put up every resistance I could muster. Dad was almost convinced when Mother came to my rescue.

50

To You, My Grandchildren

"Now J.D., he has worked hard all week at the radio station and deserves a break," she insisted. Hooray for mothers! "I'll take his place at the barn today," she volunteered. At last my dream was coming true.

Before the day was over, I negotiated a sale for the cows and began my retirement from farming. Sometimes I think life was less complicated back then.

To You, My Grandchildren

Earl Nightingale and Attitude

I can alter my life by altering my thinking. I discovered that truth in 1966, the year I became employed at WBMC Radio in McMinnville.

Bud Godwin and I were the morning duo at the station Monday through Friday. He played the current country hit records. My job was to gather and report the local news.

One particular morning was a turning point in my life. Following my 7:30 a.m. local news report, I casually walked downstairs from the second floor studios to the newsroom. Normally I would have settled into my chair, picked up the telephone and immediately begun to search out leads for some future news stories. This day, however, I turned on the station monitor (a speaker connected to the transmitter) to listen to what was being broadcast. Bud was introducing a daily radio program, "Changing World with Earl Nightingale." Our station featured this nationally syndicated five-minute program each weekday morning. I knew we included the Earl Nightingale program in our station's format, but I had never really listened to it before.

Once Bud made the introduction, a distinctive voice said, "This is Earl Nightingale. Do you know that you can alter your life by simply altering the way you think? I'll be back in a minute to explain, so stay tuned."

His voice and his question had me spellbound. I could hardly wait for the commercial to end so the program could resume. He came back on the air to explain how a person becomes what he thinks about. He even quoted words from the Bible: A man is as he thinks in his heart.

The show and its message hooked me on listening to Earl Nightingale. I even collected scripts of the shows to get the names of books suggested by Earl Nightingale to help in developing a positive mental attitude.

During the next four years while working at WBMC, "Our Changing World" became a regular part of my life. I presently have many audio tapes by Nightingale, considered to be a pioneer in motivational and inspirational materials.

To You, My Grandchildren

Earl Nightingale has since died, but I'm sure his contributions will live forever. He certainly helped to change my world. Today is the first day of the rest of my life.

To You, My Grandchildren

Ann

Have you ever wondered how many people are wearing a mask to disguise their true self? Is it because they don't like who they are? Could their present state be so unpleasant that the mask provides an escape from reality?

I believe most of us prefer putting our best foot forward in order to be accepted by our peers. I also believe that whatever we constantly think about is what we will become. To put it another way, *what we see is usually what we get.*

This line of thinking takes me back to 1970 when I was working at WJLE Radio in Smithville. Even Television programs such as *Alfred Hitchcock Presents* and *The Twilight Zone* could not produce a more bizarre story than the one involving me.

It began with a telephone call from Ann, who described herself as a daily listener in Cookeville. After complimenting my show, she requested her favorite song. Loyal listeners called regularly. Ann became a regular, but something was different about her. With each telephone visit, Ann shared more and more about her life. Her father had been a successful attorney, now retired. Her mother was deceased. She lived with her father, mainly because of his failing health and her need for moral support following a tragic accident that claimed Ann's fiancé and left her permanently scarred. She said that listening to the radio and absorbing the songs provided much-needed therapy. She also flattered me by adding that my voice conveyed a healing balm that helped to ease her pain.

Ann's telephone calls continued over the next two years. Each call reported a changing scene. One described her father's passing, another the settlement of his estate. Financial advisors suggested that Ann invest in stocks. She chose to invest in the entertainment industry instead and purchased a television production company.

Ann apparently had the Midas touch because everything she did turned into gold and more success. I was even offered a job helping to manage her company, because as she put it, "You are the only person I can trust in this tinsel world of show business." I knew Ann only by her voice, never getting closer than the telephone.

Wouldn't you be curious about meeting Ann? I was too. She

always had excuses why we couldn't meet. She was either jetting to Paris or producing a new movie in Hawaii, and on, and on, and on. I accepted the explanations, having my own career and family to be concerned about.

Whether prompted by providence or fate, Ann's story moved into the final chapter. She called me just to say hello and began describing with glowing details the recent events in her life. "Ann, will I ever meet you?" I asked.

She paused and responded, "Yes, I'm coming to Tennessee to settle some unfinished business about my father's estate. When I get there on Thursday, I'll call." She hesitated, and then with some uncertainty, said, "Let me give you a telephone number. It's to a girlfriend's house where I'll be staying." I quickly wrote down the number, my first clue into the fairy tale life of Ann, a person who seemed to have the world on a string. She concluded the conversation by saying, "Don't call me, I'll call you."

The drama was almost overwhelming. I could not resist. Slowly, I picked up the telephone and dialed the number. No answer.

The next day I visited the telephone company and begged the manager to give me the name matching the number. He first refused, but then surprised me by saying, "Young man, I'm going to give you the subscriber's name. The story is so strange, it may be true."

I could hardly wait until Ann called again. This time I wanted to hear the real story, whatever it was. "Ann," I began, "for two years we have talked. I have been your friend. Where are you calling from? Is your name really Ann or _____?" There was total silence. It seemed to last for an hour. She began to cry, then expressed anger when I told her about my investigation at the telephone company.

"Ralph, you disappoint me," she scolded. "You betrayed me."

"Ann, I only wanted the truth!" I retorted.

The fairy tale began turning into a nightmare. Ann – not her real name – was held prisoner in a marriage filled with alcohol and abuse. The radio, the songs, the telephone calls, and the pretending were her only escape. She had lived in the storybook, and it became the truth. I never heard from her again.

Remember, *what you see is what you get.*

To You, My Grandchildren

Highs and Lows of Broadcasting

The Middle Tennessee airwaves were my home from 1965 to 1986. Some of the most memorable and the most embarrassing moments in my life were recorded during those twenty-one years in broadcasting. The high points included interviews with celebrities, reporting late-breaking news, and being the first DJ in the world to broadcast one particular song that later became number one on the music charts. John Anderson's country hit "Swingin'" debuted on my morning show at WJLE Radio in Smithville. Since both John and I lived in DeKalb County at the time, he gave me the first copy of his new album before it was released to the public. One song on the album "Swingin'" caught my ear the moment I gave it a spin on the turntable. Obviously other country music fans felt the same because "Swingin'" turned into a gold record and catapulted John Anderson to international stardom.

The most embarrassing moment in my radio career occurred during a live broadcast from Westgate Shopping Center in 1980. The merchants had joined together on that occasion to stage a big weekend promotion, complete with spectacular specials and great giveaways. They also hired me to advertise the event through a marathon broadcast from the scene.

Each merchant took a turn providing me a list of specials from his or her respective store. I advertised everything from ice cold watermelons that would make your teeth chatter to tight-fitting blue jeans and Shelter Insurance protection. One participating sponsor was a well-known barber shop, managed by a lady proprietor.

You can imagine how exhausted I became after about eight hours of continuous broadcasting, reading specials, interviewing customers and introducing records. The lady barber handed me a note listing the special from her business. I casually glanced at the paper while catching my breath from an interview. It read: FOR THE NEXT 30 MINUTES, TAKE ADVANTAGE OF THIS GREAT SPECIAL — A HAIRCUT AND BLOW DRY FOR ONLY $5.00.

My mind was numb. My mouth was dry. My tongue was tired, and what I said next was totally dumb. "Ladies and gentlemen, you will want to take advantage of a great special during the next half-hour at Corner Barber Shop here in Westgate Center. Now listen, this is your opportunity. For the next thirty minutes only, a hair cut and...a blow job for only $5.00," I stammered.

One faithful listener even stopped his tractor in the field, jumped into his pick-up truck, and drove at breakneck speed a distance of thirty miles for the special. He was a friend who just wanted to give me a hard time. The lady barber was a good sport. She saved me further embarrassment by responding to the eager customer, "Oh, I'm sorry. The special you heard was discontinued after thirty minutes—or about five minutes ago. Keep listening to your radio. You'll never know what you'll hear next."

Radio Hall of Fame

I found it enjoyable today to reminisce about some broadcasting buddies from my past.

T. Tommy Cutrer was a former personality at WSM Radio and the Grand Ole Opry, and the voice for many radio and television commercials. Tommy always discouraged me from pursuing a job at a large market station. He would say, "You are better off being a big fish in a little pond rather than a minnow in a large pond." I now agree with him. My kind of broadcasting was more personal, more down-home style, I believe, than the time and temperature disc jockeys now heard on the radio.

Bud Godwin is the morning personality at WBMC Radio in McMinnville. He and I worked together for almost four years. Bud is an interesting character who taught me to drink coffee. I never drank the "stuff" until I got the morning news job at WBMC and worked alongside Bud. He stands about five feet, six inches tall, but has a voice that would have you believe he is ten feet tall.

Billy Lee Austin is a character of characters. I gave him his first job in broadcasting at WJLE Radio in Smithville. I called Bill "The Wild Man" because of his happy-go-lucky philosophy of life. He proudly proclaimed that living is to eat, drink and be merry. I remember his diamonds, the gold chains, the boats, airplanes, and the women. He certainly practiced what he preached. I really like Bill and am pleased that I helped him get started in broadcasting.

Ben Vaughn is a cousin and one of my mentors at WBMC Radio in McMinnville. Ben and Chick Brown, the station manager, encouraged and constructively tutored me in broadcast journalism. I admired them both for their commitment to excellence in the broadcast industry and for their willingness to go the extra mile.

I also enjoy memories of some creative personalities who began their radio careers with me.

Dennis Stanley is now a manager with the *Smithville Review* newspaper.

58 Shawn Jacobs is a news reporter and personality at WMOT in Murfreesboro.

To You, My Grandchildren

Tim Harvey is a bright, talented person who now has a successful law practice in Clarksville.

Karl Smith moved on to success in radio and television broadcasting.

Dwayne Page is the news director at WJLE in Smithville. He is the most dedicated and faithful employee I have ever known. I am very proud of Dwayne, mainly because I saw him evolve from being a shy teenager into a talented, confident adult.

I hope that their lives were positively influenced by me.

Chapter 7:

Punches on Hopes, Dreams and Goals

Life can be improved through visualization.
You must envision your goals so your subconscious mind can
program them.

•

What a shame if all we believe exists is what we
can be shown.

•

See it in your mind so that others may also see it.

•

Nothing happens unless you first dream it.

•

Yesterday is but a dream. Tomorrow is a vision of hope.

•

Look to this day for its life.

•

We can't predict the future, but we can create it.

•

Maximize your mind power to achieve what you want.

•

Be sure to dream. You must want something more than what you
have today.

•

If you can conceive it, and your heart can believe it,
you can achieve it.

•

All achievement begins with an idea.

•

Use self-talk to help optimize your performance and growth potential.

•

Determine what you want, plan, stay focused, and believe.

To You, My Grandchildren

Vision is the ability to see things invisible.
•
Believe that great things will happen.
•
Believe in health and happiness.
•
Hope is a duty, not a luxury.
•
You have to dream if your dream is to come true.
•
You can accomplish far greater things than you think.
•
Build your life on hopes rather than on hurts.
•
The key to willpower is "want power."
•
Carry your goals with you always.
What you think about is what you will become.
•
Before you can be a winner,
you must believe that you can win.
•
Hope is wishing for a thing to come true.
Faith is believing that it will come true.
•
Once you admit your mistakes,
you can find a new beginning.
•
Remember, with your hopes, and not your hurts,
you must set your goals.
•
Start out each day expecting good, expecting health,
expecting happiness.
•
Do something every day that moves you closer
to your long-range goals.
•
Do something daily that takes you in the direction
of your goals.

To You, My Grandchildren

Unless you start somewhere, you will never go anywhere.
•
You have the power of choice. Decide on what you want.
•
We become what we think about.
•
You can achieve worthy goals.
•
Help others to achieve their goals.
•
Be persistent in working on your goals.
•
We can always begin again.
•
Happiness is not a goal. It is a by-product.
•
You become successful when you begin moving toward a worthwhile goal.
•
Our resources are truly unlimited because of our ingenuity. To set the world right, start with yourself.
•
You have the power to help change the world. It begins with you.
•
One reason some people never get to the top is that they never start from the bottom.
•
You cannot push someone up the ladder unless they are willing to climb.
•
It takes guts to get out of the ruts. A rut is nothing more than a grave with the ends knocked out.
•
It's not important how far we travel in a day, but how far we advance.
•
We are what our subconscious minds really believe that we are. Practice in your mind seeing yourself as the person you want to be.

Chapter 8:

Business

DeKalb Star

In the business world, a familiar saying on being successful is *find a need and fill it.* Good advice, but I've learned there is more to success than just simply supplying a consumer need. I've found out the hard way that other ingredients for success include a good business plan, solid financing or a line of credit, and associates who possess similar convictions to help make the dream come true.

I once had a dream that met the first criterion for success. My passion for that dream was such that I overlooked the other considerations I've just listed.

The story began in the mid 1970's when I discovered an interesting and honest way to make extra money. I was asked to help the Tennessee Nurserymen's Association stage their annual convention in McMinnville. "Ralph, you're in the radio business and have contact with entertainers," the president of the organization observed. "Please arrange entertainment for the event and we'll pay you." So that's how it's done in show business, I thought.

The first thing I did was call an acquaintance, John Dorris, with Monument Records in Nashville. "John, here is my budget. What can I get?" One budding star at Monument, Larry Gatlin, was unavailable for the date needed, but I was lucky to hire Charlie McCoy and Barefoot Jerry. That was easy enough. Simply book the talent at a certain fee and add 20 percent for my services. Positive Promotions, my dream that became a reality, was born.

The next undertaking by Positive Promotions, however, was to result in its demise. One day while sharing coffee with my friend, Charles Gentry, we both observed that Smithville needed another newspaper to give the *Smithville Review* some competition. We jokingly agreed that the two of us had the talent to make it happen. Charles had been advertising salesman for the *Smithville Review* for several years. He knew the merchants and their needs. I was managing WJLE Radio at the time. I also knew the advertisers; and besides, I was already gathering and reporting local news that could simply be duplicated in the newspaper. "We'll call it the *DeKalb Star* and publish weekly," I suggested. Charles was in agreement.

Later, we shared the dream with Charlie Kuhn who wanted part of the action. Our plan was decided. Positive Promotions would own controlling interest in the newspaper with stock to be sold to help finance the project. Charles was elected chairman, I was the first president, and Charlie was vice-president.

DeKalb Star had a stellar beginning, just as we planned. Investors were brought in, also according to our plans. Trouble began rearing its head after three years when advertising sales declined and reserve funds were all used to meet payroll. Creditors wanted their money, particularly the company that printed the newspaper.

I had an idea. Since Positive Promotions owned controlling interest in *DeKalb Star,* maybe the *Cookville Dispatch* would clear the printing debt we owed them by becoming the new owner of the *Star,* adding to their growing chain of newspapers. Pat Williams and his mother, Ocia, owners of the *Dispatch,* knew a good deal when they saw it, but I had to sell the other stockholders on accepting the proposal. "If the *DeKalb Star* is to be successful," I pleaded, "someone with newspaper expertise must own it." I recommended giving majority ownership to the Williams family to pay the large printing bill due them.

I was successful in selling the idea to the other stockholders, but I ultimately lost in my dream for the *DeKalb Star.* Because of his failing health and financial woes with the parent company, Pat Williams gave most of his attention to his interest in Cookeville and very little to the newspaper in Smithville. Finally, almost overnight, the doors at *DeKalb Star* were closed permanently and the equipment was moved to Cookeville. All that remained was a loan at Liberty Bank with my signature and the names of Tom Bastin and Ocia Williams on it. Ocia later filed for bankruptcy, leaving Liberty Bank with one option: get their money from Tom and me. We tried the legal system, contending that the Williams family had the equipment and legal title to the *DeKalb Star* and should be responsible for the loan. Our attorney suggested Tom and I pay the debt to protect our good names in the community. We finally agreed. I wonder if the community knows, or even cares, that I am still paying for this experience?

It is not what we avoid but what we overcome that makes us strong.

Chapter 9:

Punches on Life and
Lessons in Business

You make your decisions, then your decisions make you.

•

Work will give you more than a living. It will give you a life.

•

Six words for success: Find a need and fill it.

•

Don't work for money,
but work to help bring value into other peoples' lives.

•

Let customers play an active role in your business.
Listen for their feedback.

•

Always sell: yourself, your business, or your services.

•

The key is to build your business around the future.

•

Maintain a "harvest" mindset rather than a "get rich quick" mentality.

•

The race for quality has no finish line.

•

If you don't take care of the customer, someone else will.

•

Every job is a self portrait of the person who did it.

•

Autograph your work with excellence.

•

Look for benchmarks. Learn from the best.

To You, My Grandchildren

Network with leaders and cultivate contacts.

•

Look for opportunities and develop strategies.

•

Because the customer has a need, we have a job to do.

•

Because the customer has an urgency, we must be quick.

•

Because the customer is unique, we must be flexible.

•

Because the customer has high expectations, we must excel.

•

There is no elevator to the top. You have to climb the stairs.

•

Obstacles are disguised opportunities for creativity.

•

Be quick to praise, slower to criticize.

•

The winner has a program. The loser has an excuse.

•

Of all the human inventions, the most worthless is an excuse.

•

Because the customer has a choice, we must be the better choice.

•

Because the customer has sensibilities, we must be considerate.

•

*Because the customer has influence,
we have the hope of more customers.*

•

*Within every problem is the potential for making a
significant contribution.*

•

How we think about a problem is more important than the problem.

•

*Look at problems as opportunities to challenge your creativity
and ingenuity.*

70

To You, My Grandchildren

Sometimes compromise is the gateway to a greater way.

•

Pay attention to details and network, network, network.

•

Look at business from a customer's perspective.

•

It is good business to return telephone calls promptly.

•

Learn about the competition.

•

Think like an entrepreneur. Always look for opportunities.

•

Don't be a slave to your job.

•

The value to the customer should determine your price.

•

Everyone has something to contribute.

•

Evaluate your career path regularly.

•

Because of the customer, we exist.

•

If you were your own employer, would you be satisfied with your day's work?

•

Choose a career you love, and never work another day in your life.

•

To change something, build a new model that makes the existing one obsolete.

•

What you do off the job determines what you accomplish on the job.

•

Being a winner is inside your head.
You must have a winning attitude.

•

People are more excited about selling if they get a piece of the pie.

To You, My Grandchildren

One of the tragedies in life is a good idea killed by procrastination.
If the idea has value, do it now.

•

Justice, not generosity,
is an executive's most reassuring quality.

•

Increase your potential by empowering others to help you.

•

Organize your time for maximum efficiency.

•

Resolve to perform what you should. Perform what you resolve.

Chapter 10:
Friends and Others

Miss Ocia and the Simple Life

I have heard that the simple things in life can often bring us the deepest joy. A special friend of mine, Mrs. Ocia Carter, had a unique ability to keep life simple and in perspective.

Miss Ocia had a refreshing approach to journalism, particularly community news in the *Smithville Review*. Her weekly Temperance Hall Community news attracted subscribers for many years. Loyal readers were located in all parts of the country and even remote areas of the world.

She wrote the Temperance Hall news just like she saw it. I recall some typical articles that described the passing of a good neighbor and Miss Ocia's subsequent visit to the funeral home to pay final respects. Her account would usually read, "He was such a good soul. Bless his heart, he looked just like himself all dressed up in a blue suit lying in a beautiful copper casket. The dear under-taker really made him look natural, maybe even ten years younger. I was so proud."

Some other news from Miss Ocia's pen might read, "My neighbor, Lillie, reached home today from the hospital. The doctors removed a knot from her neck although I could never tell it had been there."

Another article might include something along this line: "My neighbor, Bessie, carried her son Billy to town last Saturday. He needed to get some medicine at the drug store on account of his bowel problems."

Miss Ocia Carter was a classic. She was also my friend. I interviewed her many times on local radio and television. She was just as interesting in those interviews as she was in writing her weekly newspaper articles.

To You, My Grandchildren

I hope society never gets so caught up in being "modern" that we miss the simple, important things in life, the ones that can bring deep joy.

To You, My Grandchildren

Reese Underwood

Thinking about simplicity in life reminds me of Reese Underwood, one of our neighbors when I was a young boy growing up in the New Home community of DeKalb County. Reese found a way to avoid stress in deciding what best to wear.

He maintained a simple wardrobe of one pair of overalls and one blue cotton shirt. He wore them every day, seven days a week, whether on the farm, in town, or at church.

Reese really took the worry out of selecting and maintaining a wardrobe. He never washed them either. Each morning, he simply put on the same pants and shirt worn the previous day.

This routine went on for at least three or four months, or until Reese decided to change. He then purchased another pair of overalls, another plain blue cotton shirt, and burned the old ones.

Remembering Reese reminds me that maybe society places too much emphasis on the attire and not enough on the person. Some people even argue that clothes make the person, and that we should dress for success.

I believe, however, that success comes from knowing and accepting who you are, and by allowing your personality to be expressed through inward expressions, not outward adornment.

To You, My Grandchildren

Ben Adamson

Another special person who made a lasting impression on me was Mr. Ben Adamson, a gentle man with a tender spirit. For over thirty years, his life was devoted to teaching young people the importance of the three R's.

He taught more in the classroom, however, than reading, writing and arithmetic. He instilled within his students the values of respect, responsibility, and resiliency. I should know because Mr. Ben was my principal and basketball coach at Cross Roads Elementary School.

He stressed honesty and integrity. I also remember him placing what I consider the proper perspective on the game of basketball. "Let's enjoy this win, but remember it's only a game." The losses were treated almost in the same manner. "It's only a game, and there are more important things in life to be concerned about. Besides, we'll get them the next time."

I visited Mr. Ben and his wife, Miss Macon, at their home in Liberty, Tennessee. We enjoyed reminiscing about Cross Roads School and basketball. He asked, "Do you remember when we won the championship?" I nodded in agreement, but I honestly had forgotten that night in 1959 when Cross Roads beat Belk by one point to claim the title as DeKalb County's top elementary school basketball team. Our roster included Don Nixon, Orvil Goodwin, Carl Ray Hale, Toy and Troy Mullican, and Tucker Hendrix. I was a reserve guard.

Mr. Ben recalled, "I put you in during the last part of the game to help us use up as much time as we could. I remember you dribbling the basketball and keeping it away from the other players."

The truth was that I was almost scared out of my shoes by having to compete with the much larger players. My strategy was simple: stay out of their way and take as much time as possible off the game clock.

At that point in our musings, Mr. Ben suddenly remembered, "I still have the trophy in my attic. Do you want to see it?"

He must have sensed my answer. Before I could mutter a word, he was up, out of the chair, and off to fetch the proof of that wonderful night in basketball history. I could hardly believe my eyes. There it was, DeKalb County Champions 1959. He asked,

To You, My Grandchildren

"Would you like to have it to keep?"

Miss Macon spoke up, "All things work together for good to those who love the Lord. Ben has been talking about that trophy and how he would like to pass it on to someone who will treasure it as much as he does."

I was speechless for a moment. Somehow I got the words out, "Yes…it's wonderful…I'll keep it…you'll never know what this means to me!"

Mr. Ben Adamson was one of my favorite teachers. Many schoolteachers may have more ability in the classroom than he did, but none in my opinion can compare to him as a wonderful human being and a gentle man.

To You, My Grandchildren

Santa Claus

Santa Claus also has had a tremendous impact on my life. He gave me something more valuable than money. Santa showed me an example of how to love. I can still hear him say, "Ole Santa is blind to color and deaf to language. I love everybody, no matter their race, creed or color."

Santa was true to his word. I saw him in action for almost ten years. He was the same humble, loving and jolly man each time I saw him.

He was rich in many ways. He was considerate, honest and loving toward all people whom he met. His heart was much bigger than his means. He lacked the resources to provide the candy and toys Santa is expected to give good girls and boys.

I met Santa in the 1970's after reading about him in a newspaper article. For some reason, I felt an urge to call him at his home in Viola, Tennessee. "Santa, you don't know me," I began, "but I believe we are supposed to meet."

His reply was a confirmation. "I need someone to be Santa's helper. You are the one," Santa said emphatically.

Who could refuse Santa Claus? Not me. "Yes, Santa I will be your helper," I agreed, "and together we'll find a way to accomplish your dream of spreading the love of Christmas." I honored my promise to Santa by calling several business friends who agreed to sponsor Santa during the holiday season.

Santa received no salary from the money we collected. It was used to purchase candy and fruit with a little left over for putting gasoline in his old white van.

During those ten years, my job was to raise the money and make the necessary purchases. Santa's job was to be Santa. We were almost inseparable from Thanksgiving to Christmas Eve, visiting schools, hospitals, nursing homes, churches, and the mentally disadvantaged.

Before Santa's arrival at each location, I would announce that a special person was about to make a visit. "Do you believe in the jolly ole man from the North Pole?" I asked. Some were believers. Some were skeptics. I then told the audience that Christmas has a special magic if a person will just have faith. "Close you eyes and listen carefully," I would encourage.

To You, My Grandchildren

You can imagine what happened next. Santa entered the room and gave his official, "Ho, Ho, Ho!" Santa captured their hearts and their imagination. Children were awed. Teenagers were amused, and the elderly appeared to be younger. Santa had a unique quality that I have never seen in anyone else.

Santa was born in Atlanta, Georgia, during the Great Depression. His father apparently could not cope with abject poverty, having to support a wife and raise a family. He left them to fend for themselves.

Santa told me about those uncertain years and how the Salvation Army provided the only Christmas he could expect. He also told me about his promise to help others by sharing the spirit of Christmas.

After becoming an adult, Santa moved to Texas where his life really changed. As he became older, Santa's hair turned gray prematurely. He also became rather pudgy, just like Good Saint Nick. Some people even said he looked like a hippy with his long silver hair and beard.

Many others had different opinions about this soft-spoken man with a twinkle in his eyes. He was soon invited to appear at Christmas parties, parades and charitable events during the holiday seasons. "That was when I became Santa and discovered my mission in life," he once told me.

He and his family later moved to Tennessee after he became physically disabled from a heart attack. That was when I met him.

My friend Santa left this world during the summer of 1986. He left me with memories that I will treasure forever. John Coker was a real Santa Claus 365 days a year. His heart was worn out from a life of giving.

To You, My Grandchildren

The Trapp Family

I read that Jennings Trapp of Smithville passed away. I am now smiling as I reminisce about Jennings, a simple man with a unique talent. He could mimic a crow by playing his harmonica and making all these strange shrills that sounded like a crow.

At most events where I was broadcasting on radio or serving as master of ceremonies, Jennings would wait in the wings hoping that I would recognize him and invite him to perform his famous "crow call."

I also remember that on a few occasions he and his wife invited me to their home. While there, they would insist that I sample a fresh coconut cake that Mrs. Trapp had prepared. They knew that coconut cake is one of my favorites.

Thinking of Jennings Trapp makes me wonder what success really is. It is hard to know. Jennings Trapp was successful in his own world, one that was simple and uncomplicated by all the frills society often associates with being successful. He was honest. Mrs. Trapp liked to make those coconut cakes. She was also successful.

The Trapps and others like them can teach us many lessons about life if we will take the time to see and hear them.

To You, My Grandchildren

Gertrude Owen

Over twenty years as the master of ceremonies at the DeKalb County Fair in Alexandria provided me some interesting experiences. I started my volunteer career at the DeKalb County Fair in 1970 when the Smithville Jaycettes asked me to announce the Fairest of the Fair beauty pageant.

My voice has been heard announcing such events as mule and livestock shows, tractor pulls, walking horse competitions, and musical presentations. One of the most interesting projects was announcing the annual baby show, mainly because of my dear friend, Gertrude Owen.

I don't believe anyone else could have more passion for organizing a baby show. Her heart was in the right place, but age affected her organizational skills. I laugh to myself every time I recall the many times that Mrs. Owen mistakenly registered a girl in the baby boy category, or vice versa. During one particular pageant, Mrs. Owen had a precious 16-month-old girl registered in the "prettiest twins" division.

I can almost see Mrs. Owen smiling from ear to ear. She would always give me a big hug after each baby show and remind me, "Nobody can announce a baby show like you. You make my job so easy." What she never knew was that I always double-checked her registrations, making any necessary corrections before the public was informed about the upcoming event.

To You, My Grandchildren

Bobby Gooch

There is no business like show business. I agree with the person who first said that. Earlier today, for whatever reason, I began reminiscing about some of the interesting characters I have met in show business.

I have helped coordinate and announce events that featured the talents of such notables as Charlie Daniels, Hank Snow, Tom T. Hall, Grandpa Jones, Tammy Wynette, George Jones, and many others. My favorite show biz characters, however, were amateurs who wanted to be on stage for reasons other than money.

One person in particular made a lasting impression on me. He was Bobby Gooch, a consummate rhinestone cowboy who could almost make a harmonica talk. I remember Bobby playing at the Smithville Fiddlers Jamboree. He wore gaudy costumes, complete with sequins and fringe. Bobby was also toothless and his dark hair was weighed down with a good dose of greasy oil.

Appearances can be deceiving, and Bobby was a perfect example of that truth. To see him on stage, you might think that he was just another egotist basking in whatever glory there was in winning the applause of thousands of Jamboree fans. Bobby had another reason, one he shared with me.

Bobby Gooch was orphaned at age ten. He became street smart in order to survive. That meant sleeping under bridges, in cardboard boxes, or under whatever other protection there was available. It also meant sometimes stealing in order to have enough money for the next meal. One brush with the law would forever change his fate, however. He was arrested, convicted, and sent to prison on a charge of car theft.

Is there any hope for a criminal with no education, no close relatives to offer support, and no goals in life? Bobby's answer came in the form of a counselor who encouraged him to pick up the harmonica. Learning to play was not an easy task for Bobby. Progress came slowly. After several months of practicing night after night on the mouth harp, the sounds finally started to become melodious.

Bobby found something to love, something that made him feel important, and something positive to share with the rest of the world. He vowed never again to live a life of crime.

To You, My Grandchildren

Bobby's day finally arrived, the day his debt was paid to society. "I was so happy to be free and to have my music," he once recalled to me. "I now want to use every opportunity to perform and let the world know what is inside my heart." Bobby became a traveling minstrel, moving from one festival to the next.

I later learned through a friend that Bobby was terminally ill. Apparently the illness gave Bobby more urgency to share his love for music and to give something back to society. I believe the costumes were part of his message: Be all you can be with your life.

To You, My Grandchildren

Marty Kaercher

Tonight, I began my "winding down" process for the day by assimilating some positive punches. One punch that comes to mind is that the most important things in life are not things. This punch reminded me of my good friend Marty Kaercher, whom I spoke with today. Our favorite greeting each time we are together is, "I love you more than you love me." Marty was a patient today at Middle Tennessee Medical Center being treated for a heart attack that occurred last week. I call him the Bubble Gum Man. He always has bubble gum and candy for everyone he meets. Today when I called him, I quickly said, "Marty, I love you more than you love me." He responded, "I barely have the strength to argue with you. Please pray for me."

Cousin Bobo

I was reminded earlier today of a simple, yet dynamic princi-ple of life: Always be true to yourself. To put it another way, never try to be someone that you cannot or should not be. James G. "Bobo" Driver commented on the importance of that principle while I visited with him and his wife, Nell, in Smithville.

Bobo and I called each other "cuz," a common expression for cousins or close friends. We were friends as well as cousins, indi-rectly. Actually, Nell and I are distantly related, and for many years the three of us affectionately claimed our kinship.

My first recollection of Cuz goes back to when I was about six or seven years old. Bobo and his sons, all about my age, were enter-tainers. They picked and grinned on the steps of the DeKalb County Courthouse during political rallies. I also remember their playing music for Fourth of July picnics at Colvert's Lake Resort, once a popular place in Smithville.

I became better acquainted with Cousin Bo when a small group of us began planning the Smithville Fiddlers Jamboree in 1971. Cousin Bo was a prime mover and shaker behind the suc-cessful Jamboree, now regarded as one of the top summer attrac-tions in the South. He could always be counted on to handle the important job of registering contestants, no easy task when you consider the thousands of musicians, dancers and novelty perform-ers that flocked there each year. I was the Jamboree's master of cer-emonies and program director until I left Smithville in 1985 to work at WGNS Radio in Murfreesboro.

Cousin Bo was the most detail-oriented person I have ever known. That quality is important when putting together a major event like the Smithville Fiddlers Jamboree, now attracting up to 100,000 people to a town of approximately 3,500 during the Fourth of July holiday.

Bo used his strong will and positive attitude in his final years to challenge the pain of cancer and heart disease.

While we were talking, Bo took occasion to pass a few com-pliments my way. "I believe in giving flowers to the living," he remarked. "The flowers I have for you, Ralph, are because you have remained the same person you always were." A tear rolled down his cheek. I also cried while holding his hand to show my

85

acceptance and appreciation for his sincere compliment.

In my opinion, life is a changing process. I have changed in many ways, hopefully for the better. Bo's words will always remain in my heart.

To You, My Grandchildren

My Life's Hall of Fame

A person's life is influenced through the people he meets. As I muse today, some interesting friends come to my mind.

Ben Adamson, one of my favorite school teachers, was principal and basketball coach for several years at Cross Roads Elementary School. Mr. Ben was the only teacher to ever spank me, a punishment resulting from fighting with Willard Pack.

Robert Eller is a Smithville businessman who befriended me during six years in the Tennessee Army National Guard. Sergeant Eller looked out for my best interest, especially when other sergeants tried to draft me for an assignment. Many guardsmen called him "Stone Face," but I saw in him a heart of gold.

Othel Smith was a businessman and former mayor of Smithville. His easy credit plan with no interest enabled me to purchase furniture and household appliances as an eighteen-year-old newlywed. The mayor proved to be a faithful friend.

Tom Bastin was owner of the Western Auto store in Smithville. Tom and I fought hard to keep the *DeKalb County Star* from bankruptcy. The weekly newspaper, which I helped to start, finally cost Tom and me several thousands of dollars because we chose to pay our debts. Tom and I were also partners in another activity, a lakeside ministry sponsored by the First Baptist Church in Smithville. For four years, each Sunday morning during the summer, we led singing and shared the Gospel with campers at Center Hill Lake.

Bertha Carter McBride is a good lady. I first met Bertha when she was married to Walter Carter, former owner of Carter Truck Lines in Smithville. Her children, Walteen and Joe, have been my friends since we were school age children. Bertha later married Elzie McBride, a former school superintendent and teacher. There was one occasion when Bertha literally had me buzzing. I was master of ceremonies for the annual Harvest Festival Beauty Pageant. She was my assistant. I requested that she have a glass of water under the podium to quench my thirst during the program. Bertha tricked me by placing a glass of white wine there instead. As the evening progressed, I began to feel the effects of her practical joke, but none of the pageant contestants or fans knew the difference.

To You, My Grandchildren

Franklin (Chick) Brown was my mentor during the early years in broadcasting. Chick was a plain, down-to-earth man with a creative mind and loyalty to his profession. He was the best newsman I have ever known, who could adlib for hours if necessary.

Dr. W.E. "Doc" Vanatta was my boss and president of Center Hill Broadcasting Corporation. Doc gave me the opportunity to grow creatively while I was manager of WJLE Radio in Smithville. His favorite expression to me was, "Keep us on the air and in the black." He trusted me. I remember how he almost cried the day I resigned as WJLE manager, a job I had held for fifteen years. It was almost like two family members parting company. As I left, he reminded me, "Ralph, I have given you everything at WJLE except the deed to the property."

Andrea Loughry is the epitome of what I think a lady should be. She is gracious, honest, pure in character, and a professional. She was president of the Rutherford County Chamber of Commerce in 1986 when I was employed as its executive director. Her advice and guidance will always be appreciated by me.

Loutisha Winchester was the first Sunday School teacher I remember. I honestly think that I was her favorite class member. I could tell because she usually called on me to offer prayer and take up the offering. She often used me as an example of what good little boys and girls should be. I didn't deserve her praise, but it encouraged me because I didn't want to disappoint her.

Stoney Merriman was a fellow journalist, a sidekick, and my friend. He and I traveled together several years reporting on DeKalb County High School basketball, baseball and football. Stoney paid me some high compliments when I resigned from WJLE Radio. He wrote two extensive articles in the Smithville Review commending my life and my work.

In my opinion, these special people have earned a place in my life's Hall of Fame.

Chapter 11:

Punches on Life

Life will not deny the person who gives life everything.

•

Doing things right is not as important as doing the right thing.

•

Courtesy is to a person what fragrance is to a flower.

•

Fill your mind with thoughts of joy.

•

It matters not how long we live but how well.

•

Search for knowledge as hard as you would search for a hidden treasure.

•

Pay close attention to constructive advice.

•

Do good just for the sake of doing good.

•

Accept who you are and use your talents to the fullest.

•

The best thing you can give someone is what you are, not what you have.

•

You will reap as you sow.

•

Tomorrow is a time of anticipation.
Today is a time of reflection and action.

To You, My Grandchildren

Learn to expect, not to doubt.

•

Do it now.

•

Have a definiteness of purpose.

•

Make the world a better place for the cause of Christ.

•

Constructively criticize the action but never the person.

•

Security is in the person, not in the job.

•

Your life is a masterpiece.

•

Learn something new daily.

•

Be considerate of other peoples' time.

•

The best thing to do behind a person's back is pat it.

•

Stand for something or you'll fall for anything.

•

Refuse to give up.

•

Value your own uniqueness.

•

Each individual has unlimited potential.

•

Strive to make the next hour better than this one.

•

Live this moment as if it is the last while praising God for the blessings you see.

•

Be important in the life of a child. A hundred years from now, it will matter.

•

Don't be anxious. Anxiety destroys peace of mind, creates tension, and limits creative thinking.

•

Don't get so caught up in what others expect of you that you forget who you are.

To You, My Grandchildren

Dare to paint outside the lines.

•

Remember, people appreciate "thank you" notes.

•

In all that you do, be fair to others.

•

Want to succeed.

•

Leave the world a better place than you found it.

•

Know who you are and what you want in life.

•

Try doing what some think is impossible.

•

Read. It's the way to become successful.

•

Do what you can, with what you have, where you are.

•

Dare to dream in color.

•

We learn much when we are thankful.

•

Make your life one of thanksgiving.

•

You need a purpose for your life that is greater than money.

•

Always keep faith in others, but be self-reliant.

•

Practice faith, hope and charity.

•

In everything you do, try to do it better than you did previously.

•

The easiest thing in the world is to be yourself. Don't be a phony.

•

The grass may look greener on the other side,
but it's just as hard to mow.

•

Don't get so busy keeping track of things that you miss the train.

To You, My Grandchildren

See the world in a new, exciting and personal way every day.

•

Live with confidence and enthusiasm.

•

Live this day as if it is your last.

•

It's better to admit your faults than boast about your merits.

•

Be prepared to listen, then listen to be prepared.

•

Think. It is the best way to grow richer.

•

You are responsible for yourself. Don't blame others.

•

Be thankful!

•

Don't worry about the bad news. Start making good news.

•

Others can't know you until you know yourself.

•

Don't wait for an appropriate time to do good. Do it now.

•

Practice saying pleasant things in the morning.
This will set the tone for your day.

•

It's good to talk about other people if you speak of their good qualities.

•

When you've traveled the last mile,
make sure you have meant something to someone.

•

We treat people the way we see them. Our expectations have a direct
bearing on other people's performance.

•

If doing good were a crime,
would there be enough evidence to convict you?

•

People will become what you encourage them to be,
not what you nag them to be.

To You, My Grandchildren

Strive to make the world a better place.

•

Try to profit from your mistakes.

•

Find something good in all personal relationships.

•

Put self-interest aside to work on something you believe in.

•

A good person may fall but will get back up.

•

There is no need to hurt others to gain what you want.

•

Let your praise come from others, not from yourself.

•

Hold on to the things that are good.

•

Give of yourself without the thought of return.

•

Try to make someone's life easier because you have lived.

•

Help older people feel worthy and wanted.

•

When you receive a good turn, never forget it.
When you do a good turn, forget it immediately.

•

We'll pass this way only once.
Any good that we can do should be done now.

•

Celebrate your birthday every day.
Each day should be a "new" beginning.

•

Each day, learn something new about yourself
and the world you live in.

•

Really listen to others, empathize with them and show concern.

•

Life may appear to be an uphill road. Make sure you have the
positive power in your engine to travel life's highway.

To You, My Grandchildren

We need a purpose that we can live for, a self that we can live with,
and a faith that we can live by.

•

Good mental health comes from a balanced temperament,
alert intelligence, socially accepted behavior, and a happy disposition.

Chapter 12: Lessons

On Speaking to People

I feel compelled to speak when meeting someone on the street. Also, I have the urge when entering a room full of people. I guess it all goes back to my childhood and the way I was taught. I really feel bad when I don't do it.

Earlier today, I began thinking about the importance of speaking to other people. Not only do I like to speak, but I also enjoy waving a friendly hello by gesturing with my hands and arms. I especially enjoy calling someone by their first name and then add, "My friend, my friend."

My father enjoyed speaking to people. He was even faithful in speaking to other motorists while driving. He would raise his index finger or one hand from the steering wheel. When standing face to face with someone, he usually quipped, "Hey cuz" or "Hey neighbor."

Society today doesn't encourage the art of speaking. It seems that many people are too busy to give eye contact and speak to those they meet. Maybe they are afraid that speaking denotes weakness and vulnerability when courtesy is shown to another human being.

How are future generations going to learn the value of speaking? Most children are taught, "Don't speak to strangers." My question is, if we don't speak, how can we ever become friends and make the world a better place?

To You, My Grandchildren

On Appreciating Life

Sometimes I think the "good ole days" were not so good, but they certainly taught me some valuable lessons and appreciation for life. Thinking about life reminds me of something I once heard. Living to be 70 years old represents: 24 years sleeping; 14 years on the job; 8 years being amused; 6 years eating; 6 years of being in school; 5 years in transportation; 4 years in conversation; and 3 years of convalescing.

My advice is to really experience each day. For example: Really taste the food you eat. Really listen to what family and friends have to say. Really look at the sky. Really take the time to smell the air.

This line of thinking reminds me of a friend named Charlie Matthews. He wears a watch on his left arm. I do the same, except Charlie's watch is much different from mine. His is a Mickey Mouse watch.

"I'm 44 years old and this watch reminds me not to take myself too seriously," Charlie explained. "I think it's important to keep a sense of humor and be able to laugh at myself."

Charlie made a point that I shall always remember. I also am reminded that we can get so caught up in what others expect of us that we forget who we are. It's not necessarily what we are going to do tomorrow, but what we are doing today.

To You, My Grandchildren

On Unknown Lives

Arlie Warden was 77 years old, a retired farmer. Elbert Heady, a retired factory employee, was 73. Mack Choate lived to the old age of 92. He had been a farmer and a former magistrate.

Those brief descriptions in the obituaries of tonight's newspaper left me wondering about who they were, what they accomplished, and what life meant to them. I feel saddened that I don't know more about them.

It doesn't seem enough to me that a person's life can be summarized in a simple paragraph. I would like to know what made them happy, what made them sad, what caused them pain, and what inspired them. Somehow, I wish that a person's life could be recorded in a book, one that captured every glowing detail. I think it would be interesting to compare the experiences of others to my own. Maybe I would learn more, and by learning, enjoy a deeper appreciation for the life that has been given me.

It occurs to me that each person has a book of life. Chapter One is when a life begins, but I think the book has no end.

To You, My Grandchildren

On Using Four Letter Words

Earlier today, I rummaged through a box of old papers and discovered something I wrote several years ago. It was a note written to my son, Randy Vaughn, on his 13th birthday, August 7, 1982.

My Teenage Son
Now, you're seeing life through the eyes of a teen.
Growing up will be different from your boyhood dreams.
As sure as there will be sunshine, there's going to be rain.
As certain as pleasure, there will be pain.
Life is good. This you'll discover,
Because God made you like no other.
Created in love, you were made to love.
Let love be your guide.
Share it and keep it forever at your side.
Tomorrow, when this day has passed from the scene,
You'll know exactly what I mean.
I thank God for you and the joy you have brought to my heart.
Because of Him, you and I will never part.

I remember when Randy was born at Riverpark Hospital in McMinnville. He was a large baby, weighing over ten pounds.

I recall his struggles while learning to walk and the funny sounds that later became his talk. I also remember one particular event that taught me a good lesson in childrearing.

He was about two years old at the time. It was Sunday morning, and Randy had just been bathed and dressed in his best church clothes. While his mother and I were not watching, he wandered out the unlocked back door and into the yard. Almost immediately, I suspected where he was and quickly looked out the window to see. Sure enough, he was in the back yard and headed straight to our barbecue grill.

I saw what was about to happen. "Randy, wait, I'm coming out there," I yelled. Even though I was quick on my feet, it was too late. Somehow he raised the grill hood and then proceeded to let those soot-covered hands walk all over his freshly starched, once-white outfit. "Damn it, Randy, see what you've done," I blurted out.

He looked up at me, his eyes filled with innocence. "Damn it,"

98

he echoed. I couldn't believe my ears. A two-year-old said a four-letter word. Not Randy, I must have imagined it.

I reached down, swooped him up into my arms, and silently promised to never again let him hear me say an uncomplimentary four-letter word.

To You, My Grandchildren

On Warm Fuzzies

How many times have you suddenly thought of someone and then decided to write him or her a note expressing your feelings? Those spontaneous letters and cards are wonderful. They give warm feelings to both the sender and the receiver. I call those feelings "warm fuzzies."

God apparently enjoys giving warm fuzzies, too. Have you ever driven into a crowded parking lot, circled several times, and then discovered a single parking space near the entrance? I have many times. Thank you, Lord, for Your message and warm fuzzy.

I have also driven on several occasions to a fast-food restaurant to pick up an order and received more of God's warm fuzzies. After the attendant gave the price of my purchase, I reached into my pocket and pulled out the exact change. Thank you, Lord, for Your reminder of love.

I remember one particular rainy night while leaving a doctor's office en route to my favorite drug store to get a prescription filled. I suddenly spotted an elderly lady in the parking lot desperately trying to start her stalled automobile. "May I help you?" I called out.

"My car won't start," she responded. I immediately drove my car alongside her stranded vehicle, raised both hoods, and proceeded to get soaking wet while attaching the battery cables. The lady sighed with relief when the dead engine came alive. "Young man, I want to pay you," she offered. I declined. She protested and stuck some money in my shirt pocket.

We both went our merry ways. She headed home and I drove on to the drug store. When paying for my prescription, I remembered the money she placed in my pocket. I reached in and discovered it was enough to cover my prescription right to the penny.

Thank you, Lord, for Your warm fuzzies.

To You, My Grandchildren

On Helping Others

I received a telephone call today from a businessman in Columbia, Tennessee, who expressed appreciation for my recent visit to his town. He and a group of Maury County leaders requested that I meet them and share information on a successful program conducted by the Rutherford County Chamber of Commerce.

His compliments and kindness were appreciated by me, but one particular comment made that trip to Columbia all the more gratifying. He said, "I had only one opinion about what a chamber executive director should be until you spoke to our committee." He added, "You helped to broaden my vision for the Maury County Chamber and its leadership." Wow, what a compliment!

In my opinion, there is nothing more exhilarating to the human spirit than to know something of lasting value was done to benefit another person. His comments today have started me thinking about incidents from my past.

Suddenly, I find myself back at Cross Roads School in DeKalb County. The first person to flash across the screen in my mind is Jim Bo Farris, a timid, frightened young boy, three years my junior. Jim Bo was born into an impoverished home, apparently lacking material needs as well as emotional ones like love and encouragement. He cried constantly while at school, disrupting the Little Room. Maybe someday I will know why Jim Bo took to me. My talking and reassurance apparently had a calming effect on him because the teacher called on me several times when Jim Bo refused to eat lunch or sit with other students his age. Jim Bo made it through that first year of school; but then his family moved from Cross Roads Community, and I have no idea whatever became of him.

Years later while I managed WJLE Radio in Smithville, my secretary once remarked, "Ralph, you always attract the down-and-out or those wanting a hand-out." My response then and still is, "What is the value in living if we don't have empathy for other people? Yes, there was Jim Bo. There have been others like him who needed a kind word or deed. A man destined for death without medical services but lacking the money to pay for them. A family surviving when the electricity has been cut off again. A lady contemplating suicide but deciding to call me because she heard a friendly voice on the radio.

One day I suspect that each of us will be shown the degree of influence we had on others. I have a chill thinking about it. My prayer is that the positives will be greater than the negatives.

Chapter 13:

Punches on Successful Living

You can't give anything away that you do not first possess.

•

People say they are bored when they are really bored with themselves.

•

Your last must be your best.

•

Most people never reach their full potential. It has to do with what they feel they deserve.

•

Your best opportunities are available today.

•

When you're swimming in water over your head, the depth is irrelevant.

•

You're never rich enough to lose a friend.

•

Boys and girls are born. Men and women are made.

•

The time to make friends is before you need them.

•

Who wants to be average? Average is the worst of the best and the best of the worst.

•

There have never been two sunsets exactly the same since time began.

•

It is important to know when to speak your mind and when to mind your speech.

To You, My Grandchildren

You don't have to be dull to be sincere.

•

Tact is the ability to make a point without making an enemy.

•

You and I are the future.

•

Every minute of anger loses you sixty seconds of happiness.

•

It is better to give than to receive.

•

Inspiration burns out if more fuel isn't added.

•

To thine own self be true.

•

We learn much when we are thankful.

•

If your opinion is worth anything, why give it away freely?

•

The mouth speaks what the heart is full of.

•

If you think the whole world is wrong, it may be surprising what the world thinks of you.

•

A smile enriches those who receive it but never impoverishes those who give it.

•

The person who complains that he never had a chance probably never had the courage to take a chance.

•

Every day we walk by more opportunity than we could develop in a lifetime.

•

The longer you put off something you should do, the more difficult it is to get started.

•

Life has a principle known as the universal boomerang. What you throw always comes back.

•

If you become so angry that you don't know what to do, it is better to do nothing.

To You, My Grandchildren

Those who live in stone houses should not throw glasses.

•

We can never win an argument.

•

A wise person will listen and understand reproof.

•

The more you have, the more responsible you must become.

•

If you never tasted the bitter, how could you know the sweet?

•

A little job well done is a step toward a bigger one.

•

We are wise when we are willing to learn from others.

•

A wise person is modest in speech but exceeds in action.

•

The most adorable beauty does not wrinkle with the years.

•

Take time to work, it is the price of success.

•

The sand in life's hourglass is running lower every second and can't be refilled.

•

Live each day as if it is your last and you'll have a better appreciation for time.

•

Take time to dream, it is the way to hitch your wagon to a star.

•

Knowing when to speak and when to listen is considered great wisdom and understanding.

•

One thing worse than a quitter is a person who is afraid to begin.

•

People usually project on the outside how they feel about themselves on the inside.

•

What you communicate by example is more important than what you communicate verbally.

105

To You, My Grandchildren

A lot of people don't have much to say and that's fine. The trouble with some people is that you have to listen a long time to find out.

•

Take time to think, it is the source of power.

•

Take time to play, it is the secret of youth.

•

Take time to read, it is the foundation of wisdom.

•

Take time to be friendly, it is the road to happiness.

•

Take time to laugh, it is the music of the soul.

•

Take time to love, it is the highest joy in life.

Chapter 14:

Punches on Love

Perfect love casts out fear.

•

To love others, you must love yourself.

•

There is no such thing as something for nothing.

•

Thoughts are things, and powerful things at that.

•

Greet each day with love in your heart.

•

Love is freedom, not control.

•

The deepest need of any person is the need to be needed.

•

The loving person must spontaneously touch, smile and think of others.

•

Money will buy a dog, but only love will make him wag his tail.

•

If we seek a friend without a fault, we'll remain without one.

•

If you love someone, you'll instruct them with wisdom.

•

Love wins when everything else fails.

•

Laugh often and love much.

ABOUT THE BOYS & GIRLS CLUBS

Our Mission is to inspire and enable all young people
especially those from disadvantaged circumstances to
realize their full potential as productive,
responsible and caring citizens.

This mission is reinforced by our core beliefs, which are
that Clubs provide: a safe place to learn and grow;
ongoing relationships with caring, adult professionals;
life-enhancing programs and character development
experiences; and hope and opportunity.